IN PRAISE OF LIFE

IN PRAISE OF LIFE

BY
DR. DONALD DEMARCO

🏵 ENROUTE

ENROUTE

En Route Books & Media
5705 Rhodes Avenue, St. Louis, MO 63109
Contact us at contactus@enroutebooksandmedia.com
Find En Route online at http://www.enroutebooksandmedia.com

Cover design by TJ Burdick

Front cover image credits:
tonynetone, Earth, Flikr CC- https://flic.kr/p/6EwuqM
Aaron, Embracs, Flikr CC- https://flic.kr/p/AMweE
Baby - Santiago Burdick, photo by TJ Burdick

Back cover image credit:
Clarke, Brenda, Texture/Background 13, Flikr CC- https://flic.kr/p/8TvRrw

Paperback ISBN: 978-1-950108-66-4
E-book ISBN: 978-1-63337-090-6
LCCN: 2016936352

Printed in the United States of America

ACKNOWLEDGEMENT

Many streams of thought enter the mind of an author, providing the fodder and the formula for a book. I am indebted to more people, places, events, and experiences than I can possibly recount. They remain in my debt, unnamed, but not un-cherished. Also in my debt are the editors of *The Human Life Review*, *The Hartford Catholic Transcript*, *Voices*, *The National Catholic Register*, *Social Justice Review*, *Homiletic & Pastoral Review*, *Crisis*, *Interim*, *The Wanderer*, *Celebrate Life*, *Linacre*, and *This Rock*.

This book is prayerfully dedicated to our grandchildren with the ardent hope that they will go forth in praise of the life that they have been given.

"There are only two ways to live your life. One is as though nothing is a miracle. The other is as though everything is a miracle."

— Albert Einstein

"I am the way and the truth and the life."

— John 14:6

CONTENTS

INTRODUCTION 7

I LIFE AND EVOLUTION

FIVE REASONS WHY THERE CANNOT BE LIFE   10
HAS THE BUTTERFLY OUTSMARTED DARWIN?   17
EVOLUTION AND THE BRAIN   21
PHILOSOPHY AND INTELLIGENT DESIGN   24
DID DARWIN EVER CRY?   30

II LIFE AND MEANING

LIFE IS A GIFT   36
HOW'S LIFE TREATING YOU?   39
DESTINIES AND ROADBLOCKS   42
TEN COMPLACENT MAXIMS   45
WHAT LIES BEYOND STARDOM?   48

III LIFE AND LOVE

LOVE DESCENDING   54
SHOULD THE GENERATIONS OVERLAP?   57

THE MYTH OF NEUTRALITY   60

SEVEN LEVELS OF BELONGING   63

THE BEGINNING OF LIFE   66

IV LIFE AND TRUTH

TRUTH IN A STRAIGHTJACKET   72

THE TWO TREES   75

COMPLEMENTARITY AS HENDIADYS   78

THIS AND THAT   81

IN PRAISE OF NARROWNESS   84

V LIFE AND FREEDOM

CULTIVATING FREEDOM   90

FREEDOM AND THE LAW   94

HOW RESPONSIBILITY ENLARGES FREEDOM   97

CHOICE AND REPERCUSSION   100

FREEDOM: A CHARACTERISTIC...   103

VI LIFE AND VIRTUE

SUFFERING AN OFFENSE...   110

OUR DUTY TO THOSE IN NEED   113

THE BACH TO SCHOOL PROGRAM   116

DEMOCRACY AND DESPOTISM   119

TRANSCENDING ADVERSITY   122

VII LIFE AND SEXUALITY

THE DISAPPEARANCE OF NATURE   128

DECONSTRUCTION AND THE INCARNATION   131

GENDER IN 50 DIFFERENT FLAVORS   134

WHERE HAVE ALL THE BOYS AND GIRLS GONE? 137

WHEN IS BULLYING PERMISSIBLE?   140

VIII LIFE AND MARRIAGE

THE NATURALNESS OF MARRIAGE   146

MARRIAGE AND MARKETING   149

A NEW WORD FOR THE FAMILY   152

THE END OF MOTHERHOOD   155

WHETHER INDUCED ABORTION IS AN...   158

IX LIFE AND GRATITUDE

GIVING THANKS   164

THE MYSTERY OF THE HEART   167

WHY DO WE SING?   170

THE PLACE OF GOD   173

POPE JOHN II DAY FOR CANADA   176

X LIFE AND CHRISTMAS

CHRISTMAS AND THE VIEW FROM ETERNITY   182

CHRISTMAS AS A TRANSFORMATION   185

WHAT THE ANIMALS KNEW AT CHRISTMAS   188

MY FIVE CHRISTMAS GIFTS   191

THE WHITE HOUSE'S FIRST CHRISTMAS TREE   195

INTRODUCTION

The life of each of us human beings is characterized by uniqueness, dignity and value. What is more, it is wondrous, unrepeatable, and possessing great potential. Consequently, it is inviolable. In a very real sense, our life is all we have. It is imperative, then, that we learn to treasure it so that we can live to the fullest.

Yet, we often fail to appreciate these qualities of life. Often our appreciation arrives too late, as when we reflect on the misuse of our lives, or suffer an injury or illness, or mourn the death of another. For many of us, we are too late smart, and too soon old.

The following chapters illustrate how ten different factors can improve our appreciation of life. *Evolution* prepares it, *meaning* justifies it, *love* enhances it, *truth* directs it, *freedom* crowns it, *virtue* strengthens it, *sexuality* promotes it, *marriage* shelters it, *gratitude* honors it, and *Christmas* celebrates it.

This book is dedicated to all those who have heroically defended the importance of life and have suffered ridicule and persecution for their efforts.

January 18, 2015
Kitchener, Ontario

—PART ONE—
LIFE AND EVOLUTION

"I think Darwinism as a theory explaining evolution within species is incredibly brilliant - just unbelievably, incredibly brilliant."
– Ben Stein

5 REASONS WHY
THERE CANNOT BE LIFE

1) The Law of Entropy:

The universe appears to be one vast conspiracy against the emergence of life. Astrophysicist Sir James Jeans has estimated that the number of stars in the universe is probably something like the number of grains of sand on all the beaches of the world. These stars are burning at extremely high temperatures, and throwing off their heat in a random manner so that the amount of disorder in the universe is always increasing in accordance with the Law of Entropy. As the distinguished astrophysicist, Sit Arthur Eddington has stated, "The Law of Entropy always increases—the second law of thermodynamics—holds, I think the supreme position among the laws of nature."

A tsunami will leave a coastline more disorganized than it was before. A tornado will bring extreme disorder to a grocery store. A book thrown into the fireplace will reduce the text to smoke and ashes. The universe, it is said, is running downhill as it become increasingly disordered and disorganized. The main event in the universe is stars burning out while producing a situation in which matter is more and more randomly scattered. Away from these fires, there is the unimaginable cold of space, several hundreds of degrees below zero.

It would be hard to imagine a context more inhospitable to the formation and emergence of life. Extreme heat surrounded by extreme cold and a universe heading to what scientists have referred to as cosmic death surely does not seem to be a formula for producing life. And yet there is life, despite the overwhelming odds against its appearance. Life, which demands an exceptionally high degree of organization, exists despite everything around seemingly breaking down.

2) The precise tilting of the Earth's axis:

It is most unusual for a sun to throw off a planet. Astronomers estimate that about one star in 100,000 has a planet revolving around it in the small zone in which life is even a remote possibility. Many other features other than the right distance from the sun are required, however, if there is to be life, including the precise tilting of the earth on its axis.

The earth is tilted from the perpendicular by 23.45 degrees. The precise tilting is exactly what is needed for there to be four seasons. "Axial tilt, or obliquity," writes, Astrophysicist René Heller, "is a crucial parameter for climate and the possible habitability of a planet." If the earth tilted 90 degrees, as does Uranus, the northern pole would be boiled during part of the year while the equator would get little sunlight. At the same time, the southern pole would freeze in total darkness. "It could turn out that the Earth's obliquity of 23.5 degrees," Heller argues, is a "'Goldilocks' figure for seasonality—not too extreme in either direction—and therefore ideal for complex life." Despite the odds against it, planet Earth has just the right distance from the sun and just the right tilt on its axis for life to be possible. Yet, from a mathematical point of view, the emergence of life is highly improbable.

3) The recalcitrance of water:

Most liquids have a quite simple form of behavior when they are cooled. They shrink, which is to say that their density increases. This is due to the fact that when their molecules move more slowly, they are less able to overcome the attractive intermolecular forces that draw them close to each other. As a result most liquids become more compact as the temperature lowers to the freezing pint. At the freezing point, liquids solidify.

Water, however, does not behave this way. It is one of the few liquids that actually expands when it nears the freezing point. At 3.98 degrees Celsius, its density decreases. At the freezing point it expands by approximately 9%. This explains why ice floats on water. If water became more dense on freezing, it would submerge. Thus, if water behaved "normally," many bodies of water would freeze solid in the winter thereby killing all the marine life contained therein.

If it is true that life began in the oceans, it may be that without this "recalcitrant" property of water life would never have emerged.

4) An immunological exception:

The human body contains approximately 100 billion immunological receptors. They function to protect the body against the invasion of foreign substances. They have the extraordinary capacity to distinguish between the self and the non-self in order to protect the organism from harm.

From the standpoint of the immune system, however, the female body should reject male semen as a foreign substance thereby protecting the female organism from possible harm. Yet, if this were the case, a woman would never be able to conceive, and life would have ended with the passing of Adam and Eve. The male semen carries a mild immunosuppressant that allows the woman's immune system to make an exception and permit a "two-in-one-flesh unity. The male, then is regarded as a "friend" and so are any resulting babies. This male immunosuppressant, with respect to the billions of regulatory macro-molecules that make up the immune system, behaves in a truly exceptional way. Without this exception, the transmission of life would not be possible.

5) Achieving immortality:

Mortality is built into each human being. As people age, their bodies inevitably show signs of breaking down. Death is but a matter of time. But how is it possible that when people procreate, they do not bequeath to their progeny their age? New human life begins new and fresh. When the sheep, named Dolly, was cloned, in 1996, some thought that this would be a way of achieving a kind of cellular immortality. But Dolly was born old and exhibited premature aging before she was euthanized at age 6.

Dolly was cloned using a somatic or body cell. Procreation takes place when two sex cells, a male gamete and a female gamete fuse. Here is, at least, an image of immortality since one generation after another can procreate human beings without endowing them with their own age. Offspring are truly younger than their parents. Sex cells can do something that somatic cells cannot do, namely start life over in its pristine originality and purity. Without this capacity to procreate truly new life, the human race would not have lasted more than one generation. It is a mystery as to why the sex cells can initiate new life again and again without there being any time limitation. The generations, at least from a biological point of view, can go on endlessly.

The odds against the emergence of life are staggering. Yet life exists. The forces that produce life need to escape one obstacle and improbability after another in order for life to emerge. Somehow, despite the Law of Entropy, that highly complex and beautifully unified reality of life must find a way to emerge. The Earth must be the right distance from the sun and have precisely the right tilt on its axis. Water needs to expand as it approaches the freezing point. Male semen must carry just the right immuno-suppressant at the right time and to the right place. Sex cells must be able to initiate new life as truly new. Life is, from a scientific viewpoint, totally unexpected. And yet, no one can deny its reality. Life does exist because it is formed and guided by another Life that, in spite of the odds, shows Himself to be triumphant.

Scientists continue to ponder how life—the most improbable of all cosmic occurrences—came about. Their pondering, however carries them along widely divergent pathways, like the receding galaxies. Consensus among scientists is largely a myth. The supremely confident Richard Dawkins opens his international best-seller, *The Blind Watchmaker*, with the proclamation that "Our existence once presented the greatest of all mysteries, but . . . it is a mystery no longer because it is solved. Darwin and Wallace solved it, though we shall continue to add footnotes to their solution for a while yet." Dawkins may be alone on this point (precipice, perhaps).

A far more modest approach comes from the Nobel-Prize winning physicist Erwin Schrödinger. In *What is Life?* he confesses to a discouraging paradox that all modern scientists must face. On the one hand, there is the sense that scientists are only at the beginning stage of "welding together the sum total of all that is known into a whole." On the other hand, "it has become next to impossible for a single mind fully to command more than a small specialized portion of it." The more we know the more it becomes difficult for any one person to grasp the big picture. Science *with humility* can be most admirable, though it may not be particularly commonplace.

Biologist Lynn Margolis, of the University of Massachusetts at Amherst expresses a view that is altogether at variance to that of Dawkins. In her book, *What Is Life?*, she acknowledges how little we understand about its origin and development. She pays tribute to "life: the eternal enigma". In a similar tone, Francis Crick, co-discoverer of the double-helix, states in *Life Itself* that "the origin of life appears to be almost a miracle, so many are the conditions which would have to be satisfied to get it going". "Miracle" may be a surprising word coming from a man with decided leanings toward atheism. Scientists, however, do not always stick to their science. Crick has hypothesized that billions of years ago aliens visited the earth and may have seeded it with microbes. Perhaps that most unorthodox of philosophers, Ludwig Wittgenstein, was displaying some rare wisdom when he wrote, in *Tractatus Logico-Philosophicus*, "Not *how* the world is, is the mystical, but *that* it is". There are some things that, though they give us a sense of wonder, are too hidden or too complex for either our full observation or total comprehension. Life is perhaps better viewed as a mystery for everyone to respect and enjoy than a problem for scientists to conquer and solve.

An egregious oversight among the many scientists who believe that life is the product of chance is the simple fact that chance presupposes order. While trying to show how order evolved from chance, they ignore the fact that chance proceeds from order. As Aristotle pointed out, chance is the intersection of two lines of order or causality. For example, two friends go to a grocery store to buy provisions. They are both operating according to their own specific intentions, or lines of causality. They meet. But their meeting is by chance, not design. They would not meet, of course, had they not gone to the store. Chance does not explain order, it presupposes it. It is order that makes chance possible.

Peter Singer, who is not a scientist, makes the following gratuitous statement in his *Practical Ethics*: "Life began, as the best available theories tell us, in a chance combination of gasses; it then evolved through random mutation and natural selection. All this just happened; it did not happen to any overall purpose." To label the statement as "gratuitous" is kind. Psychiatrist Karl Stern regards it as "crazy" (*The Flight From Woman*, p. 290). Are we to believe that at a certain moment in time the temperature of the earth cooled and various atoms and molecules came together in random fashion, and over the course of billions of years produced increasingly complex organisms until a being emerged who could write epic poetry, compose symphonies, paint the ceiling of the Sistine Chapel, produce the *Summa Theologica*, choose love over hatred and justice over injustice? "Such a view of the history of the world," Stern goes on to say, "has much in common with certain aspects of schizophrenic thinking."

Life has been greatly trivialized in the attempt to see it as a purely chance occurrence. There can be no doubt that this process of trivialization has been extended to human life and to the human unborn. Our life, in a fundamental sense, is all we have. We need not know exactly how life originated and developed, although the quest can be exhilarating. Its appearance, from the standpoint of empirical science, is a mind boggling improbability. At the same time, life is a simple matter from the viewpoint of an omnipotent God. The enigma of life only adds to its value. Thus, we should cherish life as we would offer hospitality to a stranger who traveled a great distance to arrive at our doorstep seeking our assistance. Life is what we have and what we share. It is our birthright, our vitality, and our contribution to posterity. Yet, do we fully appreciate our life? Perhaps G. K. Chesterton was on the mark when he said that "Life is a thing too glorious to be enjoyed".

HAS THE BUTTERFLY OUTSMARTED DARWIN?

In 1859, Charles Darwin published a book whose original title was *The Origin of the Species by Natural Selection, or the Preservation of Favoured Races in the Struggle for Life*. It is known today almost exclusively by its abbreviated version, *The Origin of the Species*.

The science of molecular biology had yet to be discovered by 1859. Therefore, neither Darwin nor any of his colleagues knew anything about the astonishing chemical complexity of all living things.

Darwin's theory of evolution has been shown to be reasonable when applied to such external features as finch beaks, horse hoofs, and moth coloration. Changes in these areas follow his notion of a one-change-at-a-time series of slight modifications. But it does not apply to highly complex biological situations where many operations must be present simultaneously in order for the organism to survive, and where the elimination of any one of these operations would be the end of the line for that organism. Darwin, himself, worried about this and stated the following in his landmark book: "If it could be demonstrated that any complex organ existed which could not possibly be formed by numerous, successive, slight modifications, my theory would absolutely break down."

Here is Darwin's Achilles Heel. Biochemist Michael Behe has done a superlative job in showing that Darwin's theory is at a loss in dealing with "Irreducible complexity". This brace of words refers to a biological situation which, if reduced by one element, would not lead back to an organism that needed to evolve one more step, but to one that could not function at all (*Darwin's Black Box*, The Free Press, 1996). Darwin's theory cannot explain the existence of a biological complexity that did not evolve by a succession of slight modifications. The evolutionary clock cannot be turned backwards one step at a time.

In Tracy I. Storer's *General Zoology*, the author states, very matter-of-factly, that "In some moths the odor of a female may attract a male for a mile or more." What are the chances that the male can sense this smell and remain insensitive to all other scents that fill the atmosphere? It is like dialing a number at random and somehow getting the one person in the world you want to contact. Life is indeed delicate, which is why it must be honored, cherished and protected. How delicate? Consider another example from the world of zoology:

The female butterfly carries a store of perfume weighing only 1/10,000 of a milligram, and she squirts minute fractions of it into the air. These scent molecules can be detected by a male seven miles away.

Here is a synchrony of factors that need to be in place at the same time in order for their purpose to be realized: 1) the production and storage of perfume in the body of the female butterfly; 2) an organ that enables the butterfly to squirt the perfume so as to release it into the air; 3) the instinct on the part of the female to know when to release the perfume; 4) the structure of the perfume molecules that allows them to remain in the air and be dispersed over a radius of seven miles; 5) the ability of the male to detect the perfume specifically; 6) the fact that the male finds the perfume attractive; 7) the ability if the male to track the per-fume to its point of origin; 8) the fact that the female will accept the male once he arrives; 9) the mating; 10) the progeny that are thereby produced.

All these factors must be present at the same time. One ele-ment in the ten cannot evolve from a previous state. If there is no squirting organ in the female, the game is over at that point. If the male finds the perfume unattractive, he has no interest in mating. If any of these ten factors is removed, the succession of factors leading to the production of offspring is broken.

Nonetheless, this butterfly illustration is even more phantas-magorical if we consider the exquisite delicacy of the perfume. One milligram = .033 ounces. 1/10,000 mg = .0000033 oz. 1 oz, then, would be equal to 30.303 mg. or 303,030 supplies of per-fume (30.303 mg. x 10,000). Let us imagine that someone could collect this butterfly perfume (there is a Japanese perfume known as Hanai Mori Butterfly Perfume) and sell it for the extravagant amount of $1,000 per ounce. 1 oz. of perfume would be enough for this female butterfly to lure 303,000 prospective mates. In ad-dition, @ $1,000 per ounce it would cost a mere $0.0033 or 3/100 cents per supply to attract one male partner. Darwin theory col-lapses under the wings of this butterly.

"Intelligent design" is a redundant expression. If there is a "design," there must be intelligence behind it. And what is "de-sign" other than the arrangement of elements for a purpose". It is difficult to believe that there is no purpose to the release into the air of the female butterfly's perfume.

St. Thomas Aquinas did not need to draw upon molecular biology to see God's hand in the designs of nature. Though written some seven centuries ago, the following words that appear in his *Summa Theologica*, retain their appeal to common sense, as well as offering a clear example of simple and timeless wisdom: "We see that things which lack knowledge, such as natural bodies, act for an end, and this is evident from their acting always, or nearly always, in the same way, so as to obtain the best result. Hence it is plain that they achieve their end, not fortuitously, but designedly." God has outsmarted Darwin and the Darwinists, but in a certain sense, so has the humble butterfly.

EVOLUTION AND THE BRAIN

"The thing from which the world suffers just now more than any other evil," wrote G. K. Chesterton, "is not the assertion of falsehood, but the endless and irrepressible repetition of half-truths." Sartre emphasized freedom, but denied morality; Freud stressed instinct, but suppressed the spiritual; Nietzsche glorified the individual, but disdained the community; Marx celebrated the community, but rejected the individual; Darwin was enamored with empirical science, but excluded metaphysics. It is an all-too common theme. G. K., himself, we are happy to note, was not speaking in half-truths.

More contemporaneously, Richard Dawkins has joined the throng of those who pitch half-truths to a naive public by separating blind chance from intelligent design. Two sentences from his best-selling book, *The Blind Watchmaker* (1986) capture the author's view about cosmic evolution, one that he has consistently maintained throughout his career: "In a universe of electrons and selfish genes, blind physical forces and genetic replication, some people are going to get hurt, other people are going to get lucky, and you won't find any rhyme or reason in it, nor any justice. The universe that we observe has precisely the properties we should expect if there is, at bottom, no design, no purpose, no evil, no good, nothing but pitiless indifference."

There are many holes in this position, but I would like to direct attention to the unsupportable notion that the human brain, to focus on a single phenomenon, could possibly have evolved by sheer chance. One of the great stumbling blocks for Darwin and other chance evolutionists is explaining how a multitude of factors simultaneously coalesce to form a unified, functioning system. The human brain could not have evolved as a result of the addition of one factor at a time. Its unity and phantasmagorical complexity defies any explanation that relies on pure chance. It would be an underestimation of the first magnitude to say that today's neurophysiologists know more about the structure and workings of the brain than did Charles Darwin and his associates.

Scientists in the field of brain research now inform us that a single human brain contains more molecular-scale switches than all the computers, routers and Internet connections on the entire planet! According to Stephen Smith, a professor of molecular and cellular physiology at the Stanford University School of Medicine, the brain's complexity is staggering, beyond anything his team of researchers had ever imagined, almost to the point of being beyond belief. In the cerebral cortex alone, each neuron has between 1,000 to 10,000 synapses that result, roughly, in a total of 125 trillion synapses, which is about how many stars fill 1,500 Milky Way galaxies! A single synapse may contain 1,000 molecular-scale switches. A synapse, simply stated, is the place where a nerve impulse passes from one nerve cell to another.

Phantasmagorical as this level of unified complexity is, it places us merely at the doorway of the brain's even deeper mind-boggling organization. Glial cells in the brain assist in neuron speed. These cells outnumber neurons ten times over with 860 billion cells. All of this activity is monitored by microglia cells that not only clean up damaged cells but also prune dendrites, forming part of the learning process. The cortex alone contains

100,000 miles of myelin—covered—insulted—nerve fibers. The process of mapping the brain would indeed be time consuming. It would entail identifying every synaptic neuron. If it took a mere second to identify each neuron, it would require 4,000,000,000 years to complete the project. What makes all of this even more astonishing is the fact that the brain is 60% fat. In addition, a person's brain, in all its unified complexity, evolved from a single, microscopic cell! The human brain is hardly what we would expect chance to produce.

It is supremely ironic that Dawkins relies on his brain to deny the implications of its unified complexity. This is like seeing yourself in the mirror and then denying that you exist. Darwin, as we noted earlier, had a problem with irreducible complexity. He admitted that his theory could not begin to explain how a complex organ could develop in any other way than by numerous successive, slight modifications. The complex structure of the brain could not possibly have developed one factor at a time until it reached trillions of factors that somehow all worked in synchrony and provided its attendant organism with the ability to cogitate and philosophize about the brain itself as well as about the entire cosmos. The notion of intelligent design is the logical complement of scientific research. It offers a truth that has the salutary merit of not being a half-truth.

PHILOSOPHY AND
INTELLIGENT DESIGN

A good indication of how important the current discussion on "intelligent design" has become is the fact that the New York Times published a contribution by none other than Christoph Cardinal Schönborn. Predictably, the Austrian Cardinal's short article, "Finding Design in Nature," received a great deal of negative criticism. By no means, however, has the Archbishop of Vienna embarrassed himself. His mind is most acute and soundly philosophical. Philosophy, in our day, does not carry anywhere near the kind of prestige that science enjoys. It is inevitable, therefore, that philosophical points will either be scoffed at or misunderstood.

Cardinal Schönborn has answered some of his critics in a recent essay (January 2006) in *First Things* under the tantalizing title, "The Designs of Science." I want to call attention to but one philosophical statement the Cardinal makes in this article that not only illustrates the philosophical tenor of his mind, but also warrants further elucidation. This is the statement he borrows from St. Thomas Aquinas: "The natural thing is constituted between two intellects" (*Res ergo naturalis inter duos intellectus constituta*).

For Aquinas, the intelligibility inherent in nature, that is, the pattern or principle of organization that renders natural things suitable objects of knowledge, is established by God the Creator.

By applying our intelligence to nature, we begin to discover or "read into" nature what God originally put there. Aquinas sees fit to remind his readers that the Latin word intelligence (*intelligere*) is composed of two parts: *intus* (into) and *legere* (to read). Hence, one uses his intelligence to "read into" something that is already there. God's intellect comprehends the whole of nature that he intelligently created, while man's intellect, which is a discovering power rather than a creative one, comes to know it, though in a piecemeal fashion.

The intellects of God and man, consequently, both mirror nature. In the words of Cardinal Schönborn, "The natural world is nothing less than a mediation between minds: the unlimited mind of the Creator and our limited human mind." In reading nature, man is learning something about God.

The great Thomistic scholar, Etienne Gilson, has said that, "The central intuition which governs the whole philosophical and theological understanding of St. Thomas is that it is impossible to do justice to God without doing justice to nature, and that doing justice to nature is at the same time the surest way of doing justice to God." Man's mind is like a camera that can take pictures of nature. Just as a camera must be designed to capture what it photographs, the human mind must be designed to apprehend the world of nature.

Suppose a person went into a haberdashery and tried on the first suit he saw and was then surprised when he realized that it fit like a glove. This might be explained as a coincidence or merely the luck of the draw. But suppose every suit in the store, despite the wide variety of sizes, fit him like a glove. This would be much more than a surprise, but surely not something that could happen by chance. Yet, as the pagan Aristotle pointed out, "The mind can know all things." A quart bottle can contain no more than a quart of ingredients, but the human intellect can contain all things. This cannot be explained on a purely material level.

One does not need to be a Thomist, however, to appreciate the astonishing fact that man's intellect is tuned in some mysterious way to the intelligible content of nature. It is simply a matter of understanding the implications of the axiom that "man is a knower." And every person, scientist or layman, is a "knower."

No less a scientific luminary than Albert Einstein, once commented that for him, the most incomprehensible thing of all is that the universe is comprehensible. The implication of his statement should be evident. How did it come to be that the mind of man and the intelligibility of the universe matched up with each other? Does it not seem that this matching was orchestrated, perhaps even pre-established by God? Einstein also commented, and rather famously, that God does not play dice with the world (*Gott würfelt nicht*). There is more to knowledge than meets the eye.

We turn on the radio, set it to a certain frequency, and receive a signal corresponding to that frequency. We know, of course, that this correspondence has been pre-arranged. The radio station transmits signals at certain frequencies. Radio receivers are designed to pick up those frequencies. The fact that a radio receiver receives certain frequencies that originate apart from the radio does not happen by chance.

The ancient Greeks were on to something when they distinguished the "microcosm" mind of man from the "macrocosm" of the world to which the mind was magnificently attuned. Man is not only a part of the cosmos, he can behold it! This special and extraordinary attunement requires an explanation that cannot be found within the material universe itself.

Similarly, if 350 relatives and friends show up at a particular time and at a particular place to celebrate a wedding, one can be sure that the attendees had been invited and duly apprised of time and place. Their joint arrival at the church did not happen by chance, but was the result of a prior arrangement. Likewise, for Aquinas and Cardinal Schönborn, the fact that the human intellect, by nature, is structured to receive the intelligible imprint that is embedded in nature, is not something that can be satisfactorily explained either by the mind or by nature alone.

The well-known cultural anthropologist, Margaret Mead had a surprising and yet illuminating experience when she was studying the life and habits of Canadian Eskimos of the far north. She happened to bring with her two copies of one of her books. The Eskimos were utterly flabbergasted when they encountered for the first time in their lives, two things that were absolutely identical. To the Eskimos, no two faces, personalities, sunsets or ice floes were ever the same. Being human, and therefore philosophically curious, they knew that there must be a third thing that explained how two separate objects could be utterly identical in appearance, page for page, word for word, letter for letter. Not having ever seen a printing press, they could only wonder what that third thing might be. But they knew, instinctively, that there must be a third thing.

Mozart, whose musical ingenuity appears to be limitless, wrote a duet for violins in which the two violinists interpret the same written note (and succession of notes) differently and yet in harmony. The score is placed on a table. When the musicians, sitting on opposite sides of the table, read the same written note, they play it in harmony. Thus, from one side of the table, the note appearing on the fourth line of the staff is played as a D. To the violinist on the other side of the table, the same note appears to him as being on the second line of the staff and consequently as a G. The D and G played together harmonize as the interval of the fifth. In this unusual way, Mozart strings together a valid melody in which the two violins are always in harmony with each other.

Mozart provides us with a musical illustration of Aquinas' notion that nature is a common medium and the focal point of two converging intellects that intellectualize the same reality in different ways that are nonetheless in harmony with one another. God's comprehension of nature is not the same as ours. The infinite and the finite are radically distinct. Nonetheless, both comprehensions are in some way ("analogically," as Aquinas would say) married to each other. The wonder of it all lies precisely in the fact of this mysterious marriage of minds (or notes in the Mozart example) occurs. Just as a musical composition implies the work of a composer, the intelligibility of nature implies the activity of an intelligent designer.

Philosophy begins in wonder. We know that the startling things we perceive must have a cause. Although we might not know how to imagine their causes, we know that they must exist. Every child reflects this instinctive realization when he asks, "Where did I come from?" In this regard, Aquinas distinguishes between two types of demonstration: from cause to effect (*propter quid*) and from effect to cause (*quia*). In the latter case we can demonstrate that something exists which produces the kind of effects we perceive, though our ideas of it may be very shadowy.

Galileo did not receive much criticism when he declared that he was "reading the book of nature." His colleague, Johannes Kepler, who formulated the three great laws of astronomy, proclaimed, "My thoughts are following Thy thoughts." Norbert Wiener, the Father of Cybernetics, reminds his fellow scientists that the laws of induction in logic cannot be established inductively, and advises them to take seriously the notion that "Science is a way of life which can flourish only when men are free to have faith." In the absence of the faith that the universe is consistently intelligible, scientists would have neither the basis for believing that their scientific pursuits would yield fruit or the motivation for expending the considerable effort that science demands.

Yet, the aforementioned scientists were expressing, in their own way, the very point that Aquinas made back in the 13th Century that Cardinal Schönborn reiterates, namely, that a third factor must exist in order to explain how man's intellect and the intelligibility of nature happen to conform to each other. This third factor, because it is not present in itself but only through its effects (like a footprint), is not an object for the empirical scientist. But if empirical scientists deny its reality as a result of a method that formally excludes it before they set to work, then, in this regard, they have crossed over from science to ideology. Hence, as the Cardinal states, "My essay was designed to awaken Catholics from their dogmatic slumber about positivism in general and evolutionism in particular." And, let us note, the alarm clock he employs is the provocative ring of sound philosophy, an enterprise that is a universal human possession.

DID DARWIN EVER CRY?

Charles Darwin, on the 24th of November 1859, published a treatise that was destined to become the foundation of evolutionary biology. Its unabridged title, nonetheless, remains not only controversial, but politically incorrect: *On the Origin of Species by Means of Natural Selection, or the Preservation of Favoured Races in the Struggle for Life.* The science of biology has advanced considerably since 1859. Darwin knew nothing of molecular biology, for example. In retrospect, Darwin's theory of chance leading to the evolution of species is as infantile as the theory of the atom as postulated by Democritus who lived from 460 to 370 BC.

No doubt Charles Darwin had occasion to cry. Had he submitted his tears to scientific analysis, however, he would have found yet another reason to believe that Divine Intelligence had an important role to play in biological evolution. In other words, had Darwin been more scientific, he would have realized that his own "scientific" theories were not all that scientific.

The tear is composed of three distinct layers. The outermost layer is oily and acts as a sealant that keeps tears from evaporating. The middle layer is aqueous and carries vitamins and minerals to the cornea. The third, and innermost layer, is mucous and helps the tear to coat and moisturize the eyes. There is no historical evidence that there were times when these layers had a different organization or contained different ingredients. Each layer does what is needed in order to keep the eye healthy. There is no evidence that they evolved by chance or natural selection. It is empirically evident, however, that they are ordered to health.

But the tear is even more subtle and wondrous. Tears contain different chemicals depending on how they were produced. The brain tells the eyes to produce just the right kind of tears for the right kind of purpose. Basal tears coat the eye on a day-to-day basis in order to keep them moisturized. Tears that result from eye irritation contain more healing properties than do the basal tears. They are also better suited to flush foreign objects out of the eye. Emotional tears, associated with sadness, joy, or stress, carry more protein-based hormones than the other two types of tears and help the body to cleanse itself from the chemical side effects of pent-up emotions.

The theory that all of these intricate and appropriate chemical changes could have come about by chance is something that strains credulity. An Italian expression comes to mind: *Non facciamo ridere i polli* (Let's not make the chickens laugh). Biological evolutionists have pointed out that most genetic mutations are actually negative in the sense that they are inappropriate or unsuitable for the organism. Human tears provide just the right chemical ingredients to perform the task that is needed. This cannot be merely the result of chance.

Aristotle stated that women cry more easily than do men. He was right. Science has shown that the lacrimal ducts of the female are larger than those of the male. At the same time, the arms of men are stronger than those of the female. The wisdom of this natural complementarity is obvious.

Whether or not Charles Darwin cried is really a moot point. Charles Dickens, on the other hand, not only cried, but was most grateful for the experience: "Heaven knows we need never be ashamed of our tears, for they are rain upon the blinding dust of earth, overlying our hard hearts. I was better after I had cried, than before—more sorry, more aware of my own ingratitude, more gentle." We might even say that tears can be the applause of the soul. "For Edgar Allan Poe, "Beauty of whatever kind, in its supreme development, invariably excites the sensitive soul to tears."

Let us say, then, that the ability to produce tears, whether to moisten the eye, flush out foreign particles, give us relief, or express gratitude, is a gift of God. Thank God for tears. They cleanse our body as well as our mind and spirit.

—PART TWO—
LIFE AND MEANING

"At some moment I did answer yes to Someone or Something, and at that hour I was certain that existence is meaningful and that my life in self-surrender had a goal."
– Dag Hammarskjold

LIFE IS A GIFT

The great Doctor of the Church, St. Thomas Aquinas, made the thought-provoking comment that "one difference between Christ and other men is this: they do not choose to be born, but He, the Lord and Maker of history, chose His time, His birthplace, and His mother." Christ chose to be born so that He could tell those who could not make that same choice, that life is indeed a great gift, one that we should cherish and enjoy. He came voluntarily into the world at Christmas to tell us to rejoice that we were born, and to provide the light we need so that we can value our life and share it with others. He chose to be born so that we could choose to be reborn. His physical birth prepared the way for our spiritual rebirth.

Philip Van Doren Stern is hardly a household name. Yet a short story he penned on the back of a Christmas card provided moviemaker Frank Capra with material for a cinematic classic that has won an honored place in the homes and hearts of countless theater-goers and television- viewers each year at Christmas time. It is a story that forcefully impresses itself on us how utterly wrong it would be for a person to wish he was never born.

When Capra first read Stern's "The Greatest Gift: A Christmas Tale," he exclaimed, "That's the story I've been looking for all my life." Out of this long sought after story he produced "It's A Wonderful Life". As a work of art, it has been favorably compared to Charles Dickens' "A Christmas Carol". As a film, it won five Academy Award nominations. As a heartwarming story, it has become widely esteemed as *the* Christmas movie.

The story centers on George Bailey, a good man who, because of financial difficulties, finds himself at the end of his tether. He decides to do away with himself. In Stern's original story, George Pratt, in his moment of desperation, cries: "I'm stuck here in this mud-hole for life - a small-town bank clerk. I never did anything really useful or interesting, and it looks as if I never will. Sometimes I wish I'd never been born!"

George Bailey reiterates these despairing words, "I wish I'd never been born!" However, in a surprising turn of events, they summon help from on high. An angel, who is hoping to earn his wings, reveals to George how important his life was to so many others by showing him how much worse things would have been had he never been born. He is given the gift to see how indispensable and, in fact, how wonderful his life really has been. Not to be born would have effaced all the good he had done, good that he somehow had forgotten about. George is spiritually reborn and returns to his family with renewed appreciation and excitement.

The movie greatly amplifies and enriches Stern's short story. The tyrannical and parsimonious Mr. Potter, who is the very reincarnation of Ebenezer Scrooge, threatens to take possession of Bedford Falls, a folksy town located somewhere in New York State. George Bailey--played by Jimmy Stewart, who delivers the most impassioned performance of his impressive career--gives Potter no quarter: "You sit around here and you spin your little webs and you think the whole world revolves around you and your money! Well, it doesn't Mr. Potter! In the, in the whole vast configuration of things, I'd say you were nothing but a scurvy little spider!" Potter can neither own nor hire the intrepid George

Bailey, so he decides to destroy him.

As the beleaguered George Bailey edges toward despair, it appears that Mr. Potter might succeed in his treacherous scheme to close the Bailey Building and Loan (on Christmas Eve) and turn Bedford Falls into a garish Babylon.

Thanks to the help of Clarence Odbody, Angel Second Class, George is given a harrowing vision if what life in Bedford Falls would be like had he never been born. "Strange, isn't it?" says the amiable Clarence, "Each man's life touches so many other lives, and when he isn't around he leaves an awful hole, doesn't he?" "You see," he tells George, who is now beginning to realize the significance of his gift of life, "you've really had a wonderful life. Don't you see what a mistake it would be to throw it away?"

This endearing Christmas tale invites us to ask a larger question, "What would the present be like if Christ, who warmed and chastened innumerable hearts throughout history, had never been born?" The question touches upon the very meaning of Christmas.

We are often tempted, like George Bailey, to see more obstacles in our lives than opportunities. At such times, we need a light that helps us to see that our life is truly a great gift. Christmas is that light. And that light never ceases to shine.

How's Life Treating You?

The question, "How's life treating you," is one we hear often enough. And, as is the case with many commonly heard statements, it is philosophically far richer than what it may appear to be on the surface. In fact, it holds the key to that vexing and perennial philosophical question, "What is the meaning of life?"

"How is life treating you" presupposes a distinction between your *life*, which you are experiencing, and *you* who are the subject of your life's experiences. You are, in some way, prior to your life. Life is somehow external to you and imposes itself on you in ways that you may not like. Your life is not always what you want it to be. Indeed, it often seems alien to you, almost as if it were an enemy. In times when life opposes your reasonable plans or even assaults you, you may very well ask the question, "What is the meaning of life?"

In more philosophical language, there is, therefore, a distinction between my *being* and my *life*. My *being* is like a small craft set in a sea that can be, at times, calm, and at other times, quite stormy. We all recognize this precarious situation and that is why, upon greeting each other, we often ask, "How are you?" "How is it going?" or "How is life treating you?" We see each other as potential victims of life's vicissitudes and offer our sympathy and solicitude.

Life may imperil my being. On the other hand, it may awaken in me a strong desire to safeguard my being and even to respond to life's difficulties by strengthening and developing it. According to the great poet, Johann Wolfgang von Goethe, "Talent is nurtured in solitude; character in the stormy billows of the world." In his classic, *The Revolt of the Masses*, existentialist philosopher José Ortega y Gasset enlarges the point: "The difficulties which I meet with in order to realize my existence are precisely what awaken and mobilize my activities, my capacities. If my body was not a weight to me, I should not be able to walk. If the atmosphere did not press on me, I should feel my body as something vague, flabby, unsubstantial."

Viktor Frankl's universally acclaimed book, *Man's Search for Meaning*, is a reflection on how people can develop character under the most horrendous conditions, specifically, in his case, those of Auschwitz. For the noted psychiatrist, "What man needs is not a tensionless state but rather the striving and struggling for some goal worthy of him." In other words, the difficulties of life are intimately bound up with its meaning. Dr. Frankl beautifully encapsulated his philosophy by stating, "What is to give light must endure burning."

Just as a strong opponent challenges an athlete to train hard and develop appropriate skills, the challenges of life can arouse in us a determination to transcend life's obstacles and become a more complete person. John Keats, in a celebrated letter he wrote to his family two years before he died, drew a distinction between a "*mere intelligence*" and a personalized "*Soul*". "Do you not see how necessary a World of Pains and troubles is," he wrote, "to school an intelligence and make it a soul?" We inhabit, according to the great lyric poet, a world whose purpose is the art of "*soul-making*" where "the heart must feel and suffer in a thousand diverse ways."

We know that it takes a great deal of pressure to produce a

diamond. In a similar vein, personality is formed in the existential crucible of meaningful stress.

What, then, is the meaning of life? It is to arouse people from lassitude and goad them into becoming an authentic person--a "soul," in Keats' terminology; "meaning" for Frankl; self-realization for Ortega; "character" for Goethe—in which one's being begins to approximate what it was intended to become – a fully developed person. For the Christian, the Way of the Cross is the path to one's personal perfection.

DESTINIES AND ROADBLOCKS

Before St. Thomas Aquinas was born (early in 1225) a holy hermit known as Buono journeyed to the Castle of Rocca Secca, near Naples, and made a great prophecy to Countess Theodora, the wife of Count Landulf of Aquino. While pointing to a picture of the founder of the Dominican order, he said: "Lady be glad, for you are about to have a son whom you will call Thomas. You and your husband will think of making him a monk in the Abbey of Mount Cassino (Benedictines), where lies the founder, St. Benedict, in the hopes that your son will attain to its honours and wealth. But God has disposed otherwise, because he will become a Friar of the Order of Preachers (Dominicans). And so great will be his learning and sanctity, that there will not be found in the whole world, another person like him!"

She was amazed at the prophecy, and exclaimed, "I am most unworthy of bearing such a son, but God's will be done according to His good pleasure." Despite her proclamation, she and members of her family did everything they could to deter Thomas from joining the Dominican Order of Preachers. They had Thomas imprisoned in one of the castle towers, where he suffered cold, hunger, and deprivations. His two sisters urged him to change his mind. Finally, a temptress was sent to seduce him. All efforts failed and Thomas was finally allowed to follow the destiny that God had set for him.

In the case of Aquinas, no amount of roadblocks could prevent him from pursuing the path that led to his appointed destiny. There may be no other figure in human history, other than Christ (one need think only of Herod) for whom no amount of roadblocks could prevent him from achieving his destiny. Aquinas, like Christ, is a model for parents who oftentimes try to steer their own children away from destinies that God has set for them.

A 15-year-old boy, who wanted to be a writer, showed his first story to his father. The father's violent reaction was unexpected. "No son of mine is going to be a scribbler," he said, and tore the boy's story to shreds and beat him. The father wanted his son to follow his footsteps and become a dentist. In this case, the paternal roadblock also proved ineffective. The young writer went on to pen more than 90 books, 60 of them western novels. The literary world honors the name Zane Grey, whose *Riders of the Purple Sage* became the measure to which all other westerns are measured. Destinies can be difficult o discourage. A picture of the father, wearing a stern countenance, now hangs of a wall in the Zane Grey museum.

Theologian Romano Guardini remarks in his book, *Freedom, Grace, and Destiny*. That "Destiny comes to me from outside, yet it is already present within myself." Destiny is also mysteriously interwoven with Divine Providence. But it is not without its roadblocks.

A nurse attends the delivery of identical male twins in a Michigan hospital. What thoughts might run through her head at this moment? Surely, it would be the health of the newborns, and how they might fare in the coming days. But she could not have anticipated what would transpire twenty-six years later as a result of the interweaving of destiny and providence. On Father's Day, June 15, 2014, she found herself standing in line awaiting a blessing from the very same twins, Todd and Gary Koenigsknecht, who were ordained priests in the Catholic Church on the previous day. The new priests were now caring for the soul of the nurse who cared for their bodies when they came into the world (*New York Times*, June 16, 2014).

God provides destinies. We provide the roadblocks. We should pray for the ability to discern between the two and place ourselves at the service of the former.

TEN COMPLACENT MAXIMS

Mark Strand, Pulitzer Prize winner and former U.S. poet laureate, passed away recently (Nov. 29, 2014). He was a staunch atheist, declaring that he had never met God and had never been to heaven. He said, "although there are a lot of people claiming that God is telling them what to do, I have no idea how God talks to them. Maybe they are getting secret emails." In one of his poems he imagined how it felt "to open the dictionary of the Beyond and discover what one suspected, that the only word in it is nothing." His daughter Jessica spoke for the family in saying that "We weren't a religious people, but we worshipped at the foot of culture."

Jessica's comment about worshipping at the foot of culture is most intriguing. Secular culture offers little to satisfy the deepest needs of the human soul and is surely not a fit subject for worship. What characterizes moral life in secular culture is not the Ten Commandments, but ten complacent maxims that are aimed at making life easier. The irony, of course, is that in trying to make life easier, life is made immeasurably more difficult. Not exercising is much easier than exercising, but it leads to atrophy and a host of other undesirable consequences. Not studying is less taxing than studying, but ignorance is a liability. I began to think about these ten complacent maxims that are set in opposition to God's sterner and more rewarding commands. I came up with the following:

1. All religions are equal.
2. Religion is the cause of all wars.
3. Marriage is purely a social convention.
4. Masculine and feminine are arbitrary constructions.
5. Mutual consent is all that is needed to legitimate sexual acts.
6. We must always keep an open mind.
7. Everyone has a right to his opinion.
8. Always be inclusive.
9. Do not judge.
10. Every woman has the right to choose.

Although each of these maxims may initially appear to be distinctive, they all have one thing in common. They all avoid reality, whether that reality is God, marriage, love, sexuality, truth, or objective morality. They represent a falling back, a retreat from what lies beyond their realm of presumed convenience. If God does not exist, the floor opens and everything drops into a bottomless chasm.

What does it mean to be a poet in an atmosphere of meaninglessness? Matthew Arnold, another non-believer, describes this bleak image in his poem, "Dover Beach": "the world . . . hath neither really joy nor love, not light, nor certitude, nor peace, nor help for pain." A poet may eloquently express his own despair, his "unhope," to borrow from Thomas Hardy, in a way that wins him honors and fame. It does not require faith to be miserable and famous. Art is not a source of faith. It is God who dispenses this gift. Faith enlarges our world by including God and all the gifts that bear his signature.

Christ, as Simeon foretold at the Purification, will be a Sign of Contradiction. The world will prefer to have their lives governed by complacent maxims, rather than by illuminating truths. The sword that Christ brings into the world divides those who are *for* him from those who are *against* Him. He represents the narrow path. But this narrow path, this path of grace, is the road to salvation. It is a road that does not appear on the secular map of the world.

Mark Strand has entered the "beyond". We believe that he will find therein a dictionary whose vocabulary is not confined to nothing, but is far more extensive than all the words contained in the New Oxford Dictionary.

WHAT LIES BEYOND STARDOM

At the end of each year, the Media brings to our attention a chronicle of movie celebrities whose lives came to an end during that particular year. The list of these celebrities who passed from this world in 2014 is, as it always is, disquieting. So many lives, so vibrant on the screen, now extinguished. We always experience a certain shock, along with a piercing sadness when we learn of their demise. Did not Shirley Temple, Mickey Rooney, Lauren Bacall, and Sid Caesar appear to be immortal in celluloid? Did David Brenner, Joan Rivers, and Bob Hoskins have any premonition that their lease on life would suddenly expire? We watched Eli Wallach, Robin Williams, Phillip Seymour Hoffman, and Harold Ramis, and believed that they were endowed with un-diminishable vitality. We envied all those actors and actresses that seemed larger than life. And now we know that they were not larger than life. Our envy has changed to sorrow. We are left with the strange and unexpected feeling that we, the "non-celebrities," have outlasted them.

Death is the great leveler. Celluloid immortality, if there be such a thing, is not personal immortality. Movie "stars" beguiled and entertained us. But they were not beings who belonged to the heavens. They were just like us, as it turns out – mortal, fragile, destined to pass from the earth. Their deaths bring to mind two thoughts: that the distinction between celebrity and non-celebrity is trivial; that we must renew our commitment to finding meaning in our own lives. We bid good-bye to Maria von Trapp, Mike Nichols, Elaine Stritch, and Polly Bergen, and return to our own day-to-day obligations with stronger dedication. Life belongs to the living. There are no stars, only we earthlings. These deceased celebrities, like everyone else, are placed in the merciful hand of God.

The existential philosopher, Nikolai Berdyaev has stated that "Death is the most profound and significant fact of life, raising the least of mortals above the mean commonplaces of life." If there were no death, he goes on to say, life would be meaningless and without hope. It is only through death that we can escape to a better world. "If life in our world continued forever, there would be no meaning in it." *"The meaning of death"*, for Berdyaev, *"is that there can be no eternity in time and that an endless temporal series would be meaningless."* People who merely reach for the stars are not reaching high enough.

Cinematic favorites are called "Stars" because they populate the heaven of Hollywood and therefore seem to be above us. They appear to be, as the Ancients believed stars to be, "imperishable". Their deaths prove this image to be an illusion. What we all yearn for is not stardom, but eternity. Fame is a soap bubble. Christianity teaches us about the Resurrection, which is the victory of life over death. In addition, we are less likely to mistreat our neighbors when we see them as dying, even though that point of death belongs to an indeterminate moment in the future. Recognizing each person's mortality elicits in us a certain sympathy that casts aside any possible rancor or envy that we might harbor. When we visit a person who is bedridden in a hospital, our thoughts and actions are loving and supportive. We fight each other in moments when we fail to see each other as we really are, namely, mortal beings who are destined to die.

The "bell tolls for Thee," as John Donne has reminded us. We owe each other a profound sympathy inasmuch as we are all made of the same clay and are journeying toward that presently unknown moment when time and eternity intersect. Our attitude toward others would be more Christian if we saw them as dying and established our relationship with them in accordance with both this fact and the fact of our own mortality.

We say adieu to our screen celebrities with the hope that their personal lives have earned them an eternity of everlasting joy with the God who is Life in its totality.

—PART THREE—
LIFE AND LOVE

*"There is no better exercise for the heart
than reaching down and lifting somebody up."*
– quoted from the Ligourian

LOVE DESCENDING

Aristotle believed in God. This is to his credit as a great philosopher. What he did not believe was that God could be concerned about us lowly human beings. It made sense, in a way, since there is, as St. Thomas would state many years later, an infinite distance between God and his creatures. God is eternal; human beings are made out of nothing. For Aristotle, love moved the world, but it was because everything in creation aspired to the condition of godliness. The lower loved the higher because it instinctively wanted to be better; but the higher had no advantage in loving the lower. For Aristotle love was a one-way street in a unidirectional cosmos.

The more important a person is, according to the mores of the secular world, the less likely he is to associate with people far below his station. The executive washrooms belong exclusively to the executives. CEOs have their secretaries involve themselves with the *hoi polloi*. There is room at the top only for the elite. Success can be measured in terms of the distance by which one has separated himself from the madding crowd.

Other philosophers came along and regarded God not as Aristotle's "thought thinking a thought", but as an architect, or an engineer, or a clock-maker, or a mathematician, or a force of infinite potentiality. Then there were the philosophers who saw god as a process, an evolving organism, or as a being that is consubstantial with the world. These gods were large, impressive, majestic, awe inspiring. The one thing they were not, however was loving.

All this "sensible" thinking was dramatically changed when Christ came into the world as a babe. This meant that God was indeed concerned about us human beings, so much so, in fact, that he took on human flesh and presented Himself as a child who would both give and receive love. That God is Love, is a revelation. That God had the humility to become one of us is astonishing. But, love does that kind of thing. There are no boundaries to love's generosity.

And yet, the message of Christmas does not always break into the hearts of men. We are all familiar with how Ebenezer Scrooge dismissed Christmas as "humbug". And we all feel squeamish about the Grinch's plan to steal Christmas. Alexander N. Yakovlev, in his well researched book, *Century of Violence in Soviet Russia* (Yale University Press, 2002), reveals that Nikolai Lenin ordered his henchmen "to see to it that those who do not show up for work because of 'Nikola' {Christmas} are shot."

The image of the Holy Family is at the heart of the meaning of Christmas, because mothers and fathers, despite their adulthood and years of experience, make their new born child the center of their lives. They find the descending aspect of love, most natural, as well as most gratifying. As Bishop Fulton Sheen once remarked, "Christianity came into the world because a woman was willing to make a child the center of her life." Motherhood is the epitome of descending love.

It should be noted, however, that descending love is merely a prelude to ascending love. Mothers and fathers must lower themselves, despite risking backaches, before they can raise their child. God descends into the world to pick us up and carry us to heaven. The circle is completed when the hemisphere of love ascending is mated with the hemisphere of love descending. The key that unlocks love is humility. Humility must precede elevation. Pride comes before a fall. The shepherds fell to their knees in worshipping the Christ child. It is easy to believe that when they rose to their feet again, they had a better sense of their personal dignity. We, too, because of Christmas, should feel our hearts expand and our hopes enlivened. Christmas is the day that the babe in the manger told us that He as also the God of the heavens. Thus, the universe became a tidy place in which everyone could love anyone.

SHOULD THE
GENERATIONS OVERLAP?

In his novel, *The Way of All Flesh*, 19th century satirist, Samuel Butler, raised a curious question: "Why should the generations overlap one another at all? Why cannot we be buried as eggs in neat little cells with ten or twenty thousand pounds each wrapped round us in Bank of England notes, and wake up, as the sphex [mud-dauber wasp] does to find that its papa and mamma have not only left ample provision at its elbow but have been eaten by sparrows some weeks before we began to live consciously on our own accounts?"

Butler's question may seem utterly facetious, but it does, perhaps not surprisingly, have contemporary relevance. It should be apparent by now, that children need their parents not only for food, clothing, and shelter, but also for love and moral guidance. The United Nation's Committee on the Rights of the Child, however, finds reason to disagree, especially with that form of moral guidance offered to their children by parents who are Catholic.

In its February 5 Report, the Committee expressed its regret "that the Holy See continues to place emphasis on the promotion of complementarity and equality in dignity with regard to boys and girls." Committee members fear that the notion of complementarity can lead to harmful stereotyping. The Committee also expressed its displeasure that the Church has failed "to remove gender stereotypes from Catholic schools textbooks (#27)." Although it employs the terminology of "boys" and "girls," the Report is at a loss concerning how they relate to each other. It does not regard these very terms, however, to be stereotypes in themselves.

The Committee appears unaware of the harm that contraception and abortion can bring to adolescents. They are aware only of the harm done to children that results from withholding them. Thus, "The Committee is seriously concerned about the negative consequences of the Holy See's position and practices of denying adolescents' access to contraception, as well as to sexual and reproductive health and information" (#56). In addition, "The Committee urges the Holy See to review its position on abortion which places obvious risks on the life and health of pregnant girls and to amend Canon 1398 relating to abortion with a view to identifying circumstances under which access to abortion services can be permitted" (#55). These statements are tantamount to telling the Church and Catholic parents that they should allow children to enjoy sex apart from marriage, use contraception, and obtain abortions.

One might wonder why the Committee, in its spacious liberality, balks at condoning the use of alcohol, drugs, and pornography. Apparently, in the mind of the Committee members, parenting is good for breeding, but not for raising children. And raising children Catholic style can be positively dangerous. Perhaps Catholic parents should follow the example of the mud-dauber wasp.

In a response to the Committee's Report, the Holy See issued a statement that must be regarded as the epitome of restraint. It read as follows: "The Holy See does, however, regret to see in some points of the Concluding Observations an attempt to interfere with Catholic Church teaching on the dignity of the human person and in the exercise of human freedom. The Holy See reiterates its commitment to defending and protecting the rights of the child, in line with the principles promoted by the Convention on the Rights of the Child and according to the moral and religious values offered by Catholic doctrine."

Catholic parents are not about to yield to UN politically correct bureaucrats on the critical matter of how to raise their children. The UN Committee's blindness to the value of Catholic morality, which is grounded in love, is exceeded only by its blindness to the direct harm that contraception, sexual experimentation, and abortion can impose on young adolescents. Nor is the Church about to capitulate to a set of recommendations that have no basis in fact and are utterly inimical to Catholic teaching founded by Christ and refined over a period of slightly more than 2,000 years. The UN Committee is grandstanding. More to the point, however, is the fact that its recommendations, if carried out, would be in violation of the rights of children, specifically because they are in violation of the rights and duties of the parents to raise their children properly.

The Myth of Neutrality

No one comes into this world in a mode of neutrality. From the zygote stage on, there is a pulse that presses and propels us toward a more complete form of life. Imbedded in the very being of all us is a charge, an inclination, an appetite for an end. The Greeks called it an "entelechy," a force within us that impels us to something higher, to seek a fulfilling finality. Aristotelian/Thomistic philosophy is "teleological," built on the notion that all living things are naturally ordered to an end that is consonant with the needs of their being. In this sense, as T. S. Eliot has remarked, "Our end is in our beginning".

There is a marvelous French adage: *"L'épreuve le plus croyable pour l'existence de l'eau, c'est le soif"* (The best proof for the existence of water is the presence of thirst). "I do not doubt," Johann Wolgang Von Goethe wrote in 1829, "that there is life in the hereafter because it is in the order of nature that an entelechy cannot disappear." The lungs need air, and air surrounds us; the body needs food, and food is present in abundance. The eye responds to light, the ear to sound. The mind is ordered to truth, the will to what is good. Intimations of the end are grafted in our being and the various facets of our being cannot be neutral towards their respective ends. The best proof for the existence of immortality is our desire for it that is present in our souls.

Neutrality is a myth. We are positively inclined to life just as we are negatively disposed toward death. The English poet and playwright, Joseph Addison (1672-1719) encapsulated the former in the opening of his poem, *Cato's Soliloquy*:

It must be so—Plato thou reason'st well—
Else whence this pleasing hope, this fond desire,
This longing for immortality?

The desire for immortal life is not based on a choice. It is ineradicably present in us long before we ever make a choice. Likewise, happiness is not an object of choice. It is truer to say that happiness chooses us rather than to say that we choose to be happy. We cannot be neutral about being happy. A pitcher may choose to throw a fastball or a curve, but he is not indifferent to whether his team wins or loses. His choices are within the context of an agreed upon outcome. Our "longing" is an entelechy; immortality is it fulfillment.

Concerning death and oblivion, Addison continues:

Or whence the secret dread, and inward horror
Of falling into nought? Why shrinks the Soul
Back on herself, and startles at destruction?
'Tis the Divinity, that stirs within us;

We are made for life. Neutrality is an existential heresy. Therefore, a Culture of Life is not something that a person simply chooses, but is the natural consequence of living in accordance with one's nature. One lives life rather than chooses it. We should *be ourselves* and in so being, we embrace life. Morality does not begin with a choice in the sense of choosing between two or more options; it begins with an acceptance, the acceptance of who we are. Our identity is not something that we can choose. It is who we are and we cannot choose to be anything other than who we are. The Jewish scholar Leon R. Kass makes the comment that "You don't have to be Jewish to drink *L'Chaim*, to lift a glass 'To Life.' Everyone in his right mind believes that life if good and that death is bad." Being *pro-life* is to be in one's "right mind". To be or not to be in one's right mind is not a valid choice. Once one is in his right mind, then he can go about choosing the particular things that he needs in order to fulfill his life.

Can we be neutral about abortion? A philosophy teacher at a secular institution tried as much as he could to be fair to both sides in presenting the abortion issue to his class. Yet, one student complained that he was making the pro-life side seem more attractive. It did not occur to this student that the pro-life side is *inherently* more attractive inasmuch as it is congruent with her being. The pro-life view casts a light than illumines the soul's entelechy. It is what water does for the thirsty.

Choice is not a primary operation, but secondary. It is selective and decides between options. What is primary is who we are as unique individual persons. It is a given, not something to be selected. Being pro-life is being in touch with oneself and on the way to richer and more gratifying experiences of life. To begin with a disposition of neutrality is to begin in a moral vacuum and get nowhere. We lift our glass "to life" because life embraces us, not as a choice, but as a gift. Authentic living, then, begins in a mood of gratitude.

SEVEN LEVELS OF BELONGING

The dictionary is not a very good teacher of philosophy. Its definitions are limited and fail to show the wondrous versatility of the word. Philosophy, on the other hand, loves analogies, metaphors, shadings, and nuances. Moreover, it likes to put the various meanings in order. Consider the word "belonging". The dictionary fails to reveal its breadth and how its various meanings are all connecting with each other and form a ladder that ascends from the humblest to the highest. The following seven levels of belonging illustrate the dictionary's need for philosophical explication.

Position: On the humblest level, the jigsaw puzzle offers us a good illustration. "Where does this piece belong?", someone asks. Its peculiar shape and contour indicates that there is but one position that answers the question. And so, we put the puzzle piece exactly where it belongs and enjoy of small glimmer of satisfaction.

Possession: Because the puzzle is my puzzle, it belongs to me. It is my possession. It is one of the many things that I own. This level of belongingness, of course, is one-sided since I reserve the prerogative to dispossess it and give it to another. Possessions are transferrable, as well as disposable.

Place: Shakespeare's Ulysses, in his play, *Troilus and Cres-*

sida, speaks to his troops about the supreme significance for each of his men to "stand in authentic place". We all need to know where we belong in terms of our proper place in relation to others. Center field is the right place for the speediest outfielder. The seat on the throne belongs to the king. In the bridal procession, each person is in his and her proper place. We should all know where we belong in relation to others. Jumping the cue in a theater line is properly considered taboo.

Partnership: We all long to belong. Therefore, people join groups or become members of a fraternity, sorority, or a lodge. Even the French Foreign Legion is able to attract members. Partners belong to each other and work together in order to carry out certain tasks. They enjoy the sense of belonging when they fit into a collectivity of likeminded people. In this sense, belonging means being part of something larger than the self.

Parameter: Where do I belong? Late at night, children belong in bed. When work begins, the worker belongs at his post. Because home is where the heart is, it holds a special belonging for all its members. Our town and country provide parameters within which we find a special belonging. Belonging is specific. It has its boundaries.

Personification: In the words of an old song, "You belong to my heart, now and forever." Adam and Eve belonged to each other, as do husbands and wives. Wherever there is love, there is belonging. Such a level of belonging brings great personal satisfaction. It is characterized by equality and mutual assistance. This level of belonging makes it especially clear that we are not mere individuals, but belong, in some way, to others or to someone special.

Pacification: In St. Augustine's most celebrated phrase, "Thou hast made us for Thee and our hearts will not rest until they rest in thee" (*Fecisti nos ad te et inquietum est cor nostrum donec requiescat in te*). This is the ultimate level of belonging, the level that confers a complete sense of peace. All the other levels of belonging are merely preludes to it.

Along with the need to belong is the desire for peace. The two are inseparable. None of the six lower levels of belonging should be taken as fully satisfactory in themselves. Neither possessions nor memberships nor status nor personal relationships with others can satisfy our ultimate desire for belonging. Each level brings some degree of satisfaction, but only the seventh level is fully satisfactory.

In each person, there is a secret yearning. By nature, we all long to belong.

The seven levels of belonging direct us upwards from the humblest level to the highest level of belonging. The state of no-relatedness, as psychiatrists have made clear, is unbearable. At the same time, the first six levels are proportionately unsatisfactory. We should seek the ultimate, and not be content with the preambles.

THE BEGINNING OF LIFE

I do not receive many personal letters anymore. Emails have, by and large, replaced them. But, unhappily, the missives that pass through my computer soon make their way into cyberspace and then on to oblivion. They will never be candidates for nostalgia.

The important personal letters I have received, via snail mail, record a significant aspect of my history of human relations. Somehow, like wine, they seem to improve with age. Recently, I re-read a letter mailed to me in 1984. It allowed me to re-live a cherished experience, one that, I believe, is worth relating to the world.

I was on a flight from Louisville, Kentucky to Chicago, Illinois. My co-passenger, thanks to a most fortuitous seating assignment, was a most attractive young lady. As the plane lifted skyward, I pointed to Churchill Downs, the celebrated home of the Kentucky Derby that now lay a few hundred feet below. "I know," was her polite response, "I have a horse and enjoy riding." It was an awkward beginning, perhaps, but broke the ice and led to a more personal and revealing exchange.

People can be surprisingly candid on air-flights. My new acquaintance revealed that when she was seventeen and pregnant out of wedlock, medical personnel and several of her adult friends advised abortion. They intimated that being saddled with a child would be the "end" of her life. She told me about a poem she wrote that represented how she worked through her difficult decision in favor of life. Her advisors, she concluded, were misleading her. The choice she had to make was not about the *end* of life but a *beginning.*

Neither of us wanted to terminate our relationship with the termination of our flight. We exchanged letters. I had asked her if she could send me her poem. She complied. Although she felt that her literary effort was "not professional by any means," I judged it differently. Coming from the province of the heart, it made her, in my view, a poet laureate. I recited it subsequently at a pro-life banquet talk in her neighboring state of Tennessee.

> My life I did review
> At that point changes were needed I knew
> There's so much out there for us to see
> And so much of me that needs to be.
> I know it must be done on my own
> Sometimes though, I'm frightened of being alone
> This is going to be my big task
> But of Life, this I have to ask
> They all say it's not a beginning, it's the end
> But I see it a different way my friend
> I'll do it so I'll never again have to run
> At least I've started, we've begun.

It has been said the "poetry is a beautiful way of remembering what it would impoverish us to forget." I will not forget a certain teenager's courage and faith to give birth to a child in the face of fierce opposition. She regards her daughter as "truly my gift from God, who has taught me love, unselfish giving, trust, hope and most of all my child has saved my soul for life with God forever." While so many people these days regard a child as a burden, my friend saw her daughter as not only a blessing, but a Godsend who was even instrumental in saving her soul. She chose a twin beginning by affirming the start of her child's life and the dawn of her own motherhood. This is the very meaning of conception. At the Annunciation, Mary accepted both the beginning of Christ's life as a human being and the beginning of her own maternity.

The years have flown by. We have lost touch. I sometimes wonder how she and her daughter have fared. She closed her letter promising to keep me and my family in her prayers and signed it "co-passenger from Louisville to Chicago". I like to think that we are co-passengers from earth to heaven.

I sent her a copy of a book I wrote, entitled, *The Shape of Love*. She reported having enjoyed it and being "refreshed by reading how we all truly need to love and be loved." I think that God was also a co-passenger on that flight. God sends thousands of people into our lives. As well, we are sent into the lives of countless others. They and we can be momentary ambassadors of His Love. And although we may not know the ultimate outcomes of our providential meetings, we can leave the accounting to God and await the happy results which will be revealed in the next life.

—Part Four—
Life and Truth

"Truth is confirmed by inspection and delay;
falsehood by haste and uncertainty."
– Tacitus

TRUTH IN A STRAIGHTJACKET

In 1933, the Bavarian minister of education, a certain Hans Schemm, delivered the following message to an assemblage of university professors: "From this day on, you will no longer have to examine whether something is true of not, but exclusively whether or not it corresponds to the Nazi ideology."

These of professors of education were told that they should no longer dedicate themselves to searching for the truth of things, but to serve the Party with unquestioning commitment. Something higher than truth had been discovered, though it would eventually plunged the world into a nightmare of unprecedented proportions. Herr Schemm's order would make teaching a lot easier for the professors, but could they any longer be called educators?

For Saint Paul, "The wisdom of the world is foolishness to God" (1 Cor. 3:19). Truth serves everyone indefinitely; the Party ideology serves no one, and for a very short term. The dethronement of truth is like a deliberate blindness, putting everyone at a disadvantage. "The most drastic symptom of the dethronement of truth," writes Dietrich von Hildebrand, "is the way that contradictory opinions are accepted in submission to the command of the Politbureau [government]" (*The New Tower of Babel*). We are naïve today if we think that truth has been restored to its proper seat on the throne. Human beings remain foolish and what they deem progress is often foolishness writ large.

There has been much publicity in recent months concerning professional athletes found guilty of domestic violence. Various leagues have now adopted policies that respond to such incidents categorically, swiftly, aggressively, punitively, and decisively. Domestic violence is considered intolerable and reprehensible. But is it, in all its various forms?

The National Organization of Women may applaud the world of sports for taking such decisive steps to punish and curtail incidents of this abominable crime, but is it not guilty of the very same crime, and even in a far more egregious way? The word "domestic" refers to the home, where, supposedly, life should be protected from harm. The United States Constitution promises to "insure domestic tranquility". On the other hand, Carolyn Graglia makes the case, in her book *Domestic Tranquility*, that feminism, given its assault on marriage and motherhood, has robbed women of their surest source of fulfillment, which is in the home. Are secular feminists all that enamored by things that are "domestic"?

Let us free truth from its contemporary straightjacket and see the unvarnished truth about abortion. It is, though feminists would sharply disagree, an instance of domestic violence. It is a violent act, almost always resulting in death, for an unborn child that was in the domestic care of its mother. It is violence in the home, in that domestic circle that unites an unborn child with its mother.

In "The Vengeance of the Flesh," a chapter in G. K. Chesterton's book, *Eugenics and Other Evils*, the author refers to abortion as "the mutilation of womanhood and the massacre of men unborn." This is strong language and evokes the image of Herod, but it is not untrue. It is, these days, surely politically incorrect, although it is philosophically accurate. But strong language of this nature means a robust appetite for reality. The lie cannot illuminate.

Those who support life do so because they support truth.

Domestic violence, as a meaningful expression, is not confined to men against women, but includes all violent acts committed under the umbrella of domesticity, including mothers against their unborn children. An ideology--and the pro-choice movement marches under the banner of an ideology—must eliminate some element of truth. They indulge a cafeteria approach to life: some truths are acceptable, others are not. Their ideology is a checkerboard of truth and error. An ideology, therefore, is more restrictive than a consistent philosophy.

If people see abortion for what it is, an instance of domestic violence, they are more likely to see it for its reprehensible character. They are more likely to see it as an offense to women as well as an offense to the unborn. Integrity of thought in this case rests on integrity of language. If language is false, the perception of reality will be correspondingly false. The first victim in any war is truth. Yet truth is invincible and will not remain indefinitely bound by a straightjacket. Its emancipation may be slow, but it is inevitable.

THE TWO TREES

We are told in *Genesis* 2:9 that among the many trees God planted in the Garden of Eden, two were of special significance: the tree of the knowledge of good and evil, and the tree of life. God had commanded Adam and Eve not to eat the fruit of the former. There was no such prohibition concerning the fruit of the latter, although our primal parents, for whatever reason, did not partake of the fruit of that tree. There are deep mysteries associated with these trees. Nonetheless, there is fairly agreed upon consensus concerning their basic meaning. Moreover, this meaning is not only theological, attested by faith, but profoundly moral, with rich application for people of all ages.

In the *Epistle of Diogenes*, the author makes the following comment: "Indeed, there is a deep meaning in the passage of Scripture which tells how God planted a tree of knowledge and a tree of life in the midst of paradise, to show that life is attained through knowledge . . . And so the two were planted close together" (Sect. 12). Life, however, does not begin with knowledge; it is nourished and advanced through knowledge. Evidently the kind of life mentioned in *Genesis* was not biological life but a spiritual life that is indeed cultivated through knowledge. The obvious question that arises, then, concerns what reason God may have had in forbidding Adam and Eve from eating the fruit from a tree that clearly symbolizes something good.

It appears that God wanted to put his first human creatures to an initial test. Adam and Eve needed to demonstrate, through obedience, their trust in God. This was required before they could advance to the next step which involved the knowledge of good and evil. Life evolves in stages, as we well know. We must walk before we can run. Parents do not feed steak to their infant children. The immature digestive system first needs to produce the appropriate enzymes. Teachers begin math instruction with arithmetic, not with higher algebra. St. Paul speaks of the "mature" as "those who have their faculties trained by practice to distinguish good and evil" (*Hebrews* 5:14).

Adam and Eve needed to put the knowledge of good and evil in the context of trust in God. Otherwise, the great danger for them was to put trust in themselves, thereby running the risk of believing that they, and not God, determine what is good and what is evil. They needed the virtue of humility before they could safely venture into the realm of choosing good and avoiding evil. The application here to the contemporary world is evident. Abortion advocates argue that it is the pregnant woman who determines the morality of abortion and not the fact that, objectively, abortion kills a human being. Pride can blind a person to the nature of the moral act while placing too much emphasis on indiscriminate freedom.

The Tempter, in the image of a serpent, convinces Eve that eating the fruit from the tree of the knowledge of good and evil will strengthen her and make her an equal of God. He argues that God wants to keep her and her husband in a subservient position, limiting their rightful freedom. The Tempter seduces Eve into trusting him rather than God. The result, as we know, was calamitous, a Fall of tragic and prodigious proportions. Our first parents were banished from the Garden and were not able to return. They were no longer eligible to eat from the tree of life. To insure that they were kept from this tree, God "placed the cherubim, and a flaming sword which turned every way, to guard the way to the tree of life" (*Gen.* 3:24).

Just as the "life" the tree of life offered is spiritual, so too the "death" that God told would come to those who ate from the tree of the knowledge of good and evil is also spiritual. The Culture of Life and the Culture of Death, therefore, have a profoundly spiritual significance. In order to enrich our own life, we must first honor the order of creation, which includes the life that God has made. The God of the New Testament commands us first to love. Through love, we advance to the next stage of enjoying "life" on a higher, more Godly plane. By rejecting His commandment, we experience a kind of "death," one that keeps us in darkness, riveted to our pride.

The struggle between the two cultures has its prototype in the allegory of the two trees. The struggle is essentially spiritual and rests on a most fundamental question: do we as mere human beings determine what is good and what is evil? Or does God make that determination? If we answer the latter in the affirmative, we begin by honoring the life that God has created, and then allow God's blessings to enrich our lives so that we enjoy life on a higher, more joyful, and more lasting level.

COMPLEMENTARITY
AS HENDIADYS

Hendiadys is a figure of speech in which two words are used to intensify the meaning of one thing. It is an ingenious form of cognitive amplification. As a Greek word, Hendiadys means "one through two" (*hen-dia-dys*). Short and sweet are two words that, when in tandem, give added strength and clarity to the notion of *brevity*. The words "spic" and "span", though rarely used separately, when linked together emphasize more effectively the notion of *clean*. Sad and lonely, high and mighty, peace and quiet, rant and rave, safe and sound, rough and ready, fear and trembling, mirth and merriment, free and easy, fun and frolic, along with innumerable other examples, employ two words to give added intensity the meaning of a single concept. If we summon a sleepyhead to "rise", our command is far weaker than when we bid him to "rise and shine", though the simple meaning, *get up*, remains the same. Hendiadys is a paradox. It makes more out of *one* by enlisting *two*.

If you tear a dollar bill in half, you will have two pieces that in themselves have no value. But if you join them together, you reconstitute a bill that has the value of $1. The two pieces complement each other, just as, in hendiadys, two words complement and strengthen each other to elucidate an integral meaning. Neither the violin nor the bow can produce music by themselves. But together they can produce music of infinite variety. Complementarity can mean completeness. It is hendiadys in action. "I-Thou" is far richer than the mere addition of an "I" to a "you". Hendiadys transcends mathematics by making *one* larger than *two*.

God's manner of creation indicates his affection for hendiadys. He created the heavens and the earth, separated the light from darkness, and distinguished day from night. This affection for hendiadys is also evident in His creation of the human being. By creating man and woman as a complementary pair, he gave added meaning to the notion of *human*. Neither a man by himself, nor a woman by herself, conveys the notion of love for another. The full meaning of a human being, then, is completed only when a man and a woman stand before each other and are united in love. In the words of Alice von Hildebrand, "The plenitude of human nature is found only in the unity of male and female."

This special complementarity is also needed in order to evince another attribute of God, namely the particular fashion in which He creates. God creates creatively, which means that He endows his creatures with the ability to participate in his creativity through procreation. Non-complementary pairs such as a man and a man or a woman and a woman, cannot procreate and therefore do not image God's particular style of creativity.

We all share in God's enthusiasm for complementarity and hendiadys. And we share it in so many ways on a daily basis. We take pleasure in matching the cup with the saucer, aligning the salt next to the pepper, arranging a wine and cheese party, mating the napkin to the dinner plate, combining beer with pretzels, pairing the soup to the sandwich, or finding the right tie to go with the shirt. Sympathy pours forth more efficaciously when it is companioned with tea. Ham and eggs spells breakfast more decisively than ham or eggs alone. And, as the song says, love and marriage go together like a horse and carriage.

Complementarity is often derided because it seems to indicate that one person needs another in order to be complete. Thus, it creates the impression that one person alone is in a weakened state. But the truth of the matter is that complementarity, just as hendiadys amplifies one through two, rescues a person from solitude and makes him more complete. Complementarity does not weaken, it uplifts. It also underscores the fundamental significance of love and creativity. The counterpart to "It is not good for man to be alone," is that complementarity is good for man since it helps to make him whole.

THIS AND THAT

Richard Dawkins, primarily noted for his works that deny the existence of God, has stirred a lively controversy recently in offering his opinion about unborn children diagnosed with Down syndrome: "For what it's worth, my own choice would be to abort the Down fetus and, assuming you want a baby at all, try again." This view is hardly original. Peter Singer offered a similar view in his 1995 book, *Rethinking Life and Death: The Collapse of Our Traditional Ethics*. "We may not want a child to start on life's uncertain voyage if the prospects are clouded," he wrote. "Instead of going forward and putting all or effort into making the best of the situation, we can still say no, and start again from the beginning."

Dawkins and Singer would be making perfect sense if they were talking about commodities. It is not ethically problematic to return a defective appliance to the store and have it replaced with one that is in good working condition. When the dessert trolley comes along, the diner might say, "No, I don't think I will have this one. I will have that one instead." But human creatures are not commodities. Each individual human being is "this" human being and that is all he will ever be. There is no replacement human being either conceived or yet to be conceived, that can assume the individual identity of the one he is assumed to replace. When God

81

creates a new child, he is giving the parents "this" child.

By accepting the view of Dawkins and Singer, not only is the "defective" child looked upon as a commodity, but also the "replacement" child. In other words, no child has an intrinsic right to life; his life is dependent on the will of someone else, someone who is not God. God does will the existence of the child he creates and in creating that child endows it with an intrinsic worth and right to be. Dawkins and Singer are both atheists, so that the notion of God does not enter into their thinking. But in trying to justify the abortion of defective babies, born or unborn, they, by the same stroke, reduce all others to commodities. In doing injustice to some, they do injustice to all. The "replacement" is just as much a commodity as the "replacee".

Archimedes said, "Give me a lever long enough and a fulcrum on which to place it, and I shall move the world". This was achievement through power. The novelist Joseph Conrad said, "Give me the right word and the right accent and I will move the world". This was achievement through persuasion. If there is a single word that characterizes Christianity, it is love. If there is a single word that characterizes a particular philosopher it belongs to a 13th century Franciscan philosopher by the name of John Duns Scotus, and the word he coined is *haecceitas*, translated into English as "thisness". For Scotus, each being had a singularity and an existence that was all its own. It was "this" and not "that". "Thisness" is what gives a thing its individuality and identity. As far as human beings are concerned, my *haecceitas* is what differentiates me from all other human beings. Because of my "thisness", I am irreplaceable.

The notion of "thisness" needs to be restored. Each one of us is an irreplaceable "this" one. It is my "thisness" that grounds me in reality and gives me my uniqueness. No one can take my place. No one can take anyone's place. In baseball, a pinch-hitter may be a better hitter than the batter he replaces, but such a replacement is on the level of an activity, not on the ground of one's being.

There is another sinister consequence to the Dawkins/Singer philosophy. If no one is truly himself, truly a unique person, then he cannot be loved, for love is directed to the unique self. The reasons proposed for aborting defective children extends to aborting the dignity of all human beings and leaving them unlovable commodities that may or not replace others who are their inferior in one way or another. My only hope is to be a "this," and I cannot be a "that".

IN PRAISE OF NARROWNESS

In Matthew 7:13-14 and in Luke 13:24, we read about a person who comes to Jesus and asks, "Lord, will those who are saved be few?" The question anticipates a numerical type of answer and is one that is raised more out of curiosity than out of a genuine concern for moral guidance. The response Jesus gives is more profound than what the questioner is seeking: "Enter by the narrow gate; for the gate is wide and the way is easy, that leads to destruction, and those who enter it are many."

This response was, no doubt, disappointing to the questioner. At the same time, had Jesus given him a percentage that was very high, it could have engendered complacency, one too low could have caused despair. Jesus buttressed his counsel by adding, "For the gate is narrow and the way is hard, that leads to life, and those who find it are few." We should not think of salvation in terms of statistics, but by being true to our specific calling.

The word "narrow" must have been just as disagreeable in the time of Jesus as it is today. It seems embedded in the human condition for people to want things to be broad, open, spacious, and easy. When we are told that the way is "narrow," we cringe at the realization that it will also be hard. Christ came to save us, not to make things easy for us. We are already too easy on ourselves.

G. K. Chesterton has remarked that a man is rather foolish who complains that he "cannot enter Eden by five gates at once". In the same vein, Chesterton states that "Keeping to one woman is a small price for so much as seeing one woman," and that "Polygamy is a lack of the realization of sex". What we need and what serves us best may seem unduly narrow to some people, but that indictment reveals a lack of appreciation for what is appropriate and just. If we stretch the rubber band too far, it will break. If we widen the strike zone so that every pitch is a strike, it would make the "strike zone" meaningless and the game of baseball unplayable.

There is a time-honored adage that the study of law sharpens the mind by narrowing it. It is not the way of law to multiply the number of suspects and then, in a flamboyant gesture of broad-mindedness, convict all of them. Rather, the way of justice is to narrow the field of suspects until the one person is discovered who is guilty of having committed the crime in question.

Justice, like all thinking, is a narrowing activity. In thinking, we clear away the wrong solutions until we find the one that is right. It is not beneficial to place error and truth together on the same path. Thinking clarifies precisely because it narrows. It is like gardening that gets the weeds out. This process may be difficult, even laborious, but it is rewarding. The reason we begin to think is because the number of possible solutions is too great. Thinking marries the mind not to fantasy, but to reality.

In Dostoevsky's *The Brothers Karamozov*, Father Zossima says to a woman who has little faith: ". . . love in action is a harsh and dreadful thing compared with love in dreams." This instruction also falls on disappointed ears. In our dreams, love is easy and life is broad. Such dreams, however, do not convey wisdom. Life is hard and the way is narrow. But this is not what we want to hear. Surely in today's world, in trying to make marriage broad and divorce easy, we lose sight of the meaning of marriage and inevitably sap its strength.

The saintly Father Zossima, like Jesus, is not trying to be disagreeable, but only to make great things possible. The narrow gate opens, ultimately, to the expansiveness of Heaven. The wide approach contains contradictories and is doomed from the start to dissolution. The narrow way is purged of its destructive elements. Wisdom is rare, foolishness is rampant. The right answer is unique, the wrong answers are innumerable. God is One, the devil is legion. Narrowness is not to be shunned because it seems limited. It should be welcomed when it represents purity, and therefore, enhanced possibilities.

Jesus wants us to flourish. He is telling us that we must be patient. We cannot attain Heaven in a single bound. We must begin at the beginning and proceed by utilizing only the things we need. And even though this way is "narrow," it is immensely fertile and opens to ever-expanding realizations of life. On the other hand, the way that is wide and easy continually narrows until it reaches a dead end. We observe this among the licentious who are misled into thinking that their liberality is enriching. In truth, their lawlessness leads to their self-destruction.

Jesus offers us a great paradox: the narrow gate opens to a wide and satisfying life; the wide gate narrows to the point of despair. We are wise to abandon our fear of anything narrow, simply because it is narrow, and follow His instruction.

—Part Five—
Life and Freedom

"To be really alive, to be holy, one needs discipline, artistry,
– and a little foolishness."
– Abraham Heschel

CULTIVATING FREEDOM

As any horticulturalist knows, you cannot cultivate roses merely by plucking weeds and killing aphids. One must plant rose seeds. No matter how hospitable the garden is for the cultivation of roses, if there are no seeds, there will be no roses. Negative horticulture is, in itself, unproductive.

This simple, incontrovertible notion has direct applicability to human beings and their desire for freedom. No amount of negative freedom, removing barriers that would inhibit the cultivation of freedom, will ensure the cultivation of positive human freedom. This latter freedom must grow from an interior seed which is the human will.

The modern world has expended considerable effort in its attempt to clear away various barriers that appear to be obstacles to freedom. The Enlightenment sought to free reason from faith, believing that faith is an obstacle to freedom. The Marxists were committed to liberating man from the oppression of the ruling class. Freud wanted to free man from his restricting inhibitions, Darwin from the illusion that man was unique among animals. Friedrich Nietzsche was passionately dedicated to ridding the world of a non-existent God whose specter prevented man from becoming truly himself. None of these attempts to enlarge human freedom, however, all being negative, contributed one iota to the cultivation of positive freedom which is indispensable for the proper fulfillment and flourishing of the human person.

The distinguished theologian Hans Urs von Balthasar has made the observation that "human beings only become truly human when they have chosen and actuated themselves in freedom; when the 'nature' in them has been totally and freely appropriated and responsibly worked through." No one can choose freedom for us. Freedom must be willed from the inside in order for the seed of freedom to germinate. Yet, the modern apostles of negative freedom continue to have their appeal since they promise to deliver an automatic freedom, one that can be attained without personal effort. The notion of "freedom fifty-five," therefore, has become very popular inasmuch as it represents the anticipated enjoyment of freedom simply because one has been emancipated from the work force. Modern emancipatory movements will continue to have more influence than is justified as long as people neglect the more important freedom that requires effort and discipline, along with a realistic sense of one's self and one's place in the world.

The issue of freedom is being hotly contested at present in American society. In order to shed some valuable light on the issue, Cardinal Timothy E. Dolan, Archbishop of New York, has produced an eBook entitled, *True Freedom: On Protecting Human Dignity and Religious Liberty*. There can be no freedom without a recognition of the positive value of human dignity. The Cardinal refers to a number of examples that indicate a "rampant disregard" for human dignity: the approval of embryonic research, the torture of prisoners, abortion, the dismissal of the meaning of marriage, and the federal contraception mandate. "We can see, writes the Cardinal, "that there is a loss of a sense of truth and objective moral norms—rules of conduct that apply always, to everyone." Instead of grounding morality in the Natural Law, which is valid and liberating for all people, society has substituted "pragmatism, utilitarianism, and consumerism," all of which have no higher goal than the satisfaction of individual preferences.

Human dignity is an essential value. It cannot be disregarded. Indeed, justice demands that it be accorded its appropriate freedom. Human dignity is a moral value. Laws are not just that violate human dignity. Citing Pope Benedict XVI, the archbishop of New York pointed out that the separation of law from morality "fails to recognize the full breadth of human nature, and in fact both diminishes man and threatens humanity." Cardinal Dolan is indicating that laws that violate human dignity, no matter how much they appear to make people free (the freedom to be relieved of an unwanted pregnancy through abortion, for example), contribute to the Culture of Death.

If negative freedom continues unchecked, there comes a point when there is nothing left to remove. Removing every factor that appears to be a restriction on freedom--the Natural Law, faith, inconvenience, any reference to God, and unwanted human life--does not allow the person to flourish, it suffocates him. Roses will not grow, as we mentioned at the outset, by plucking weeds and killing aphids. But here, the negative horticulture is at least opposing the enemies of roses. We are not talking about their benefactors: water, soil, and sunlight. In our present situation in America, what is at risk is actually beneficial to the flourishing of the human being – the positive freedom that is concomitant with human dignity.

People would be gravely mistaken if they viewed the Cardinal's eBook as exclusively Catholic. The archbishop of New York is addressing all human beings and underscoring the essential importance of their human dignity. He is appealing to the interior core of the human person, that capacity to choose the positive freedom that allows him to flourish precisely as a person. It is a journey worth undertaking. As G. K. Chesterton once said, "If seeds in the black earth can turn into such beautiful roses, what might not the heart of man become in its long journey toward the stars?"

FREEDOM AND THE LAW

It is most interesting to me how much information about our present culture can be packed in a single snippet of news. In March of 2013, an Oklahoma woman was arrested for trying to sell her two young children via Facebook. She claimed that she needed the money to spring her boyfriend from jail. What first struck me when I read of this incident is how the gap between technology and morality seems to be widening. Rev. Martin Luther King, Jr. described it well: "The means by which we live have outdistanced the ends for which we live. Our scientific power has outrun our spiritual power. We have guided missiles and misguided men." It may be argued that this woman from the Sooner state, as well as her boyfriend, and the prospective purchasers are all somewhat misguided. We may place some of this aberrance on a culture that encourages the separation of freedom from lawfulness.

The computer, including Email and Facebook, is an achievement of unquestioned intellectual genius. Progress may belong to science, but can it also be said of morality? The computer, in so many ways, has made life more convenient for people. At the same time, the wide world of the web can turn people into electronic abstractions in their relationships with one another. How does this Oklahoma woman view her two children? Are they offspring from her flesh? Or are they commodities to be bartered away or sold? How do they appear to potential buyers on Facebook? Are they consumer objects to be acquired? What kind or relationship other than monetary does the seller have with the buyer? The intimate, personal love that children crave and need can be easily lost in the alluring light of economic gain.

The brave new world of reproductive technology has done much to make offspring appear to be commodities. Even gametes are offered for sale. One particular website, in the interest of producing more beautiful children, auctions eggs from supermodels and sperm from super-males to the highest bidder. The notion that a child is the incarnation of his parents' love is giving way to a world of freedom wherein marriage, love, commitment, and the nuclear family, have been reduced to options.

Technology brings about more freedom, but can human morality keep pace with an ever-widening field of choices? The purpose of law is to safeguard people from the negative effects of immorality. But can the law protect people from the illicit activities they arrange through the Internet? It is indeed a strange attitude wherein a person would accept the equation "$1,000 = 2 young children = bail money to release a prisoner". The equation sign creates false identifications while denying the inestimable value of human beings. The law also protects people from acts of desperation. Money seldom if ever solves deep personal problems.

Furthermore, is the willingness to pay $1,000 sufficient to qualify for adopting and raising two children? Just as the children can be reduced to commodities, prospective child-raisers can be reduced to consumers. The law is instituted to protect people. What laws will protect the children? Is freedom of choice outpacing the law?

Let us imagine that the Oklahoma mother carries out her plan successfully. She sells her children and uses the money to free her boyfriend. But this is not a happy ending. Where does this leave them? Both have little regard for the children. They may resume their relationship, but it was purchased at the expense of compromising the very interpersonal qualities that are necessary for a good relationship. It leaves them unrepentant and unreformed. They may continue to believe that there is nothing wrong with placing price tags on children, even their own.

Our computer culture has brought about an array of new problems that should inspire us to develop a better moral appreciation of the primary significance of authentic human relationships. It bears repeating to say that the computer is only a tool and was never intended to serve as a light that guides us through life. If we have made an idol of this technology, it becomes all the more important to return to a more authentic life among the living. This, too, is a way of being pro-life.

HOW RESPONSIBILITY
ENLARGES FREEDOM

There are well-known experiences we all share that have names that are not at all well-known and can rarely be shared. For example, who has heard of "Zymurgy's First Law of Evolving System Dynamics"? Yet it refers to something that we have all experienced. Its more prosaic description reads as follows: Once you open a can of worms, the only way to recan them is to use a larger can. This principle is exemplified in the title of an old standard: "How ya gonna keep 'em down on the farm (after they've seen Paree)?" "Those who labour in the earth are the chosen people of *God*," wrote Thomas Jefferson. The mass migration from farms to the cities in early 19th Century America was like opening a can of worms.

This "law" may have interesting and far-reaching personal implications. Legalizing abortion is opening a can of worms. People love freedom. Once they are set free from one confinement, they do not want to return to it. The ideology of "choice" has allowed women to enlarge their freedom. They are most reluctant to give up this freedom and go back to the time when abortion was illegal. Is it possible to enjoy more freedom and yet eschew abortion?

Let us use our imagination, now, and think of the can of

worms as a can of freedoms that are joined with responsibilities. In this case it becomes possible to accept additional freedoms, but in a context of responsibility in which choices expand without including the choice for abortion. Thus, responsible people could have more freedom on personal, social, and economic levels while these new freedoms would not include the choice for abortion. In fact, the freedom not to abort can be viewed as a higher freedom than the one that leads to abortion. A sense of responsibility can ensure additional freedoms that freedom alone cannot provide. It takes a higher kind of freedom to be forgiving, courageous, faithful, and wise. Responsibility is a catalyst that provides more freedom, not less.

Pro-lifers encourage people to be more loving and respectful toward each other. Consequently, they stress the importance of chastity in sexual relations, and justice and kindness in all interpersonal encounters. At the same time, they promote social agencies such as Birthright that helps women who have problem pregnancies to find the freedom that allows them to give birth to their unborn children. Finally, pro-life advocates recognize the need for social justice in the economic sphere and work to implement more equitable ways of distributing capital. These are ways in which the responsible use of freedom can bring about more freedom. The irresponsible use of freedom does not represent freedom at its best. Pro-lifers are on the side of the responsible use of freedom.

"Opening a can of worms," of course, has an immediately pessimistic implication. But when we consider responsibility rather than worms, the cloud clears and the horizon is bright with promise. Once a child is born, he cannot be returned to the womb. He has been admitted to a larger world, one that demands much more of him. The philosopher Arthur Schopenhauer wrote of the "crime of being born". But that is because, given his pessimistic limitations, he saw birth as opening a can of worms.

The same can be said of marriage, which Woody Allen has

pessimistically described as "the loss of hope". This holy institution requires people to abandon their individualistic ways and express their new freedoms in more spacious ways that include love for one another as well as for their children. Life, it may be said, is the personal evolution from one dynamic system to one that is even more dynamic. Concomitant with this evolution is increased freedom and, at the same time, an increased sense of responsibility. The increased freedom, of course, presents the possibility of its misuse. It is critical to remember, therefore, that the larger "can" is larger not only because it represents a broader field of freedom, but also because it represents a broader range of responsibilities.

The timeless adage, "The corruption of the best is the worst," means that an increase of freedom unaccompanied by an increase in the responsible use of that freedom is not an evolution but a devolution. It is not a step forward, but a step backward. Life is a dynamic system. For the pessimist each new challenge is akin to opening a can of worms. For the moralist each new challenge is an opportunity for growth. Zymurgy's law is a comical consolation in response to life's frustrations. "Murphy's Law" tells us that "If anything can go wrong, it will". "O'Tool's Commentary" on "Murphy's Law" states that Murphy was an optimist. We may be consoled if we can attribute our failures not to ourselves but to a law of necessity. But consolation is not growth.

The Law of Christ lacks both the comical and the pessimistic. More importantly, it is practical, communal, loving, and replete with hope. It represents an evolutionary dynamic from one system to a higher system. St. Paul advises us to, "Bear one another's burdens, and so fulfill the law of Christ" (Galatians 6:2). The Law of Christ does not operate out of necessity, but enlists both our freedom and our responsibility. It is a law that we must embrace. It is a law that opens us to a better life.

CHOICE AND REPERCUSSION

Jean Bethke Elstain, an author I greatly admire, made an astute observation when she remarked that "much that comes parading through town under the banner of 'choice' is actually a new set of constraints and compulsions." "Parading" is an appropriately descriptive word since this new attitude toward choice does not come to us through a wise and thoughtful tradition. Rather, it comes whistling into town with much clang and clatter, but with little substance. "More and more women," she goes on to say, "testify that the 'choice' to abort post-amniocentesis if they are carrying a 'defective' child is nearly irresistible: they become 'bad mothers' by carrying a child to term rather than aborting it! 'Choice' and 'constraint' always go hand-in-hand." She penned these words nearly 25 years ago (*Chronicles*, October, 1989). In retrospect, she appears prophetic. Her words are truer today than they were a quarter of a century ago when she first wrote them.

Choices are not without consequences. Bad choices can have unhappy repercussions. Nature cannot be mocked with impunity; it has a way of striking back. Overeating brings on indigestion. Immoral choices are followed by guilt and regret. In the web of life, choice is not free from a multitude of things that are not directly chosen but nonetheless do reverberate. A thief in the night may think that all he is doing is obtaining his loot. But his action puts the whole town on alert.

Joyce Arthur, coordinator of the Abortion Rights Coalition of Canada complained when actress Nicole Kidman announced to the press that she was "thrilled" at being pregnant. Ms Arthur wants pregnant women to be less positive about their pregnancies: "It certainly shows any young woman watching these movies or following these celebrities that the best option is to have the baby and it glorifies that choice." The choice to abort brings with it a prohibition of any public display of maternal joy. One choice annuls another. We must not glorify choices. We want to make all choices perfectly free of any outside influence. This would mean, incidentally, the logical end of commercial advertizing. Nonetheless, this is a strange request coming from an organization that has done everything it could to influence the choice of abortion. The choice for abortion, indeed, as Elshtain has remarked, does bring with it a considerable array of constraints and compulsions.

A college student states that he hopes abortion will remain legal since he hates using the condom. Legalizing abortion leads some men to choose being less concerned about women and more concerned about their own gratification. This is hardly a victory for women's rights. Collectively, the dire consequences of abortion produce a culture war. Free choice is never entirely free. Its ripple effects, for good or for ill, can be beneficial or costly. One must take a long range view of choice and consider what conditions certain choices bring about.

When the choice to abort is regarded as a form of "care," the consequences can be catastrophic. Concerning Obama's Affordable Care Act, W. Ross Blackburn, rector of an Anglican fellowship, raises an interesting question: "When decisions about what is and what is not covered by insurance are made by an appointed administrator with a medical sheet in one hand and a balance sheet in the other, what will happen to children whose prognosis is bleak, and treatment is expensive?" (*the Human Life Review*, Fall 2012) Does it make sense to deliver a child who requires expensive medical treatment that is not covered by the Affordable Care Act? Rev. Blackburn fears that ultimately the back-alley abortion will be replaced by the back-alley birth! Will his words written in 2012 prove prophetic 25 years from now?

If abortion is not only a "right" but a form of "care," the cheaper form of care would seem to be the reasonable way to go. In Oregon, that has legalized physician-assisted suicide, situations have arisen in which Medicaid covers the suicide but not the treatment. And since poison is a lot cheaper than medical treatment, why not choose the former? The choice for physician-assisted suicide logically leads to the choice to forego life-saving medical treatment in certain instances. We should be more attentive to the choices we lose that inevitably follow the choices we secure.

"Choice" is a mesmerizing word. It suggests freedom, but can be very deceptive. It can intoxicate people so that they lose their appetite for all other values. The world is full of regret because people have discovered, to their sorrow, that they have made bad choices. Because they initially over-valued choice, they forget about the consequences of their choices, what their choices set in motion. They ignored truth, goodness, and wisdom. Choice is validated not by itself, but how well it relates to truth, goodness, and wisdom. But this triad of values does not come parading into town, instantly captivating and capturing the minds and hearts of its onlookers. Truth, goodness, and wisdom are difficult to market, which explains why civilization is difficult to achieve.

The choice for abortion has been slowly working its way to handing over the power to choose who shall inherit the earth and who shall continue to live to insurance companies. Here, in a nutshell, is the final repercussion of very bad choices. It means that the family will yield to bureaucracy. It means that a system of money will displace a community of love.

FREE WILL: A CHARACTERISTIC OF THE CHILDREN OF GOD

God created us not as puppets that He could control, but as creatures who have been given the gift of freedom. Therefore, thanks to God's benevolence, we are free to control our own lives. This freedom, of course, is limited. We cannot do things that are outside of our human capacities. And we should not do things that are contrary to God's Commandments. It is paradoxical, then, that we are most free when we act in harmony with our nature and in accordance with God's plan. Our freedom, therefore, is not absolute, but conditional.

The misuse of freedom is self-defeating. We can use our freedom for good or for ill. As a consequence, responsibility must oversee our use of freedom. Freedom is a great gift, but it must always be used responsibly. We are the trustees of our freedom and express our thanks for this gift by using it wisely. Because our freedom should be allied to God the Father, our proper use of freedom is characteristic of our childlikeness. We are children of God. Our freedom is God's gift to us. Our responsible use of that gift is our gift to God.

Nonetheless, there is a problem in the modern world concerning freedom, especially in terms of free will. The problem goes to the very heart of the question, doubting whether we human beings are at all free. This problem of whether there really is such a thing as free will has caused considerable confusion throughout the history of thought. Does man have free will? Or is free will just an illusion? When we take into account heredity, environmental influences, emotions, the role of the unconscious, peer pressure and other factors, we begin to understand how they bring the notion of free will into question. Do we choose freely, or is it the case that our choices are determined for us by forces that are not always or easily recognized? Is free will an illusion or a reality.

The reality of free will was not much of a problem for St. Thomas Aquinas. This is because he understood the will as the "rational appetite". Thus, he tied the free will to reason as a direct consequence of reason. Because we are "rational animals," we are also free. The will is the appetite that allows us to choose what reason has proposed. Therefore, we are free because we have the capacity to reason. Because no one doubts the existence of reason (we believe in science), no one should doubt the existence of free will.

Reason recognizes an array of choices. For example, when we scan a menu, we find a variety of items that may or not appeal to our reason. One item is too expensive, another is not consistent with our dietary needs, and a third does not please our palate. Then, there are items that promise to be congenial to our budget, our health, and our appetite. We make our choices on the basis of what reason illuminates. We are free precisely because we are rational. If we were simply rational creatures (without freedom) we would found find ourselves in the curious situation of knowing exactly what we want to choose but are paralyzed and incapable of making that choice. Reason and freedom are inseparable. We can choose freely because we can think rationally. Because we can use reason, we are not compelled to order something from the menu that is not good for us. This is something we all know and experience, though we sometimes have trouble putting different pieces together.

Reason itself does not pose a problem. No one questions whether we have the capacity to reason. The evidence of our rationality is everywhere. The computer alone is sufficient proof of our ability to exercise reason. Since we cannot doubt the faculty of reason, how is it possible that we can question the reality of freedom? Part of the problem lies in the fact that even though we are endowed with reason, we do not always choose rationally. We often allow irrational factors to enter the picture and influence our decisions. As St. Paul confessed, "I do not do the good I want to do, but the evil I do not want to do—this I keep on doing" (Romans 7:19).

St. Paul is not denying that he has reason or will. He is confessing that he not choosing what his reason presents to him as good. In fact, he is affirming his capacities to reason and choose, but acknowledges that he is not using them properly. A person may possess a rare and valuable painting without realizing it because the painting is covered with layers of grime and dirt. But when the accretions are removed, the true nature of the painting as a masterpiece is revealed.

Virtue is needed so that we have the moral strength to choose what reason illuminates as the right thing to do, in other words, what is good. The person who chooses rationally in this way realizes clearly that he possesses a free will. Virtue, in the form of self-possession, ensures that our reason and will are wedded together.

In summary, we have free will because we are rational beings. Aquinas correctly identifies the will as the "rational appetite". This is the simple solution to what is often a puzzling problem. We can become confused about the existence of our own freedom, however, when we fail to choose rationally. As a result of repeated irrational choices, in the case of the person who is addicted to drugs, for example, that person may be acting out of compulsion and no longer believes that he has a free will. According to a Japanese proverb, "First the man takes the drink, next the drink takes the drink, then the drink takes the man."

When we enjoy that "serenity of spirit" (*quies animi*) that Aquinas discusses, it should be clear to us that we are possessors of both reason and free will. One of the insidious effects of immoral choices is that we can cease to know who we really are. On the other hand, we come to know better who we are as a consequence of making good choices.

—Part Six—
Life and Virtue

*"Life is a grindstone. Whether it grinds us down
or polishes us up depends on us."
– L. Thomas Holdcroft*

SUFFERING AN OFFENSE IS BETTER THAN COMMITTING ONE

In the Act of Confession we acknowledge twice that we have offended God. God is all good and deserving of all our love. Offenses against Him, therefore, are offenses against love. We are commanded to love God and neighbor. When we fail in this regard, we confess our having offended God, primarily, and neighbor, secondarily. Christianity understands the meaning of being offensive in the proper perspective. Love is pro-active; sin, as a refusal to love, offends both God and man.

Society needs a moral framework. Otherwise, it sinks into chaos. But a moral framework without any reference to God, gives man a centrality that he does not deserve. Thus, the notion of being offensive is now understood as an act that is primarily directed against man. Moreover, since society does not command people to be virtuous, being offended lacks a clear and objective basis. In this way, a person can claim to be offended for any number of reasons that are entirely subjective. Certain passages in the Bible are now deemed offensive, along with many Church teachings, pro-life views, and even opening the door for someone.

It is noteworthy that the present hypersensitivity to being offended has occurred alongside of an explosion of offensive language. Oddly enough, offensive language, especially in films, does not appear to be as offensive as words that only a few years ago, were not considered offensive at all, such as "wife" and "husband". The "coarsening of America", a phenomenon that has attracted the interest of many culture critics, is unfolding independently of an epidemic of people who are offended for subjective and often trivial reasons.

Are dumb blonde jokes offensive, or are they examples of innocent humor? "I'm not offended by all the dumb blonde jokes," quips Dolly Parton, "because I know I'm not dumb... and I also know that I'm not blonde." We should all be able to poke fun at our own foibles. No one is immune to characterization. We may be easily offended because we take ourselves too seriously. "Lighten up," is good advice for the supersensitive.

If people had a good reason to be offended, it would be by the prevalence of offensive language. Yet, such language is routinely defended in the interest of realism, liberality, and freedom from censorship. "Being offended" has taken on an ideological character which precludes any form of reasoned debate. William F. Buckley, Jr. was acutely sensitive to this development. "Liberals claim to want to give a hearing to other views," he once remarked, "but then are shocked and offended to discover that there are other views." An offended party might say, as it were, "I am offended because your view is inconsistent with my ideology". In this way, a person can allow himself to be "offended" by another's defense of traditional marriage.

Placing "being offended" within an ideological context removes the issue from philosophical discussion and makes it personal. Consequently, a person can claim being hurt by another's reference to the natural law, not because the natural law is inherently offensive, but because it does not fit in to one's ideological frame of reference. In this way, photographs of aborted babies are offensive, although photographs of victims of automobile accidents are not.

We would all be better off if we concentrated on doing good, rather than in looking for ways to be offended. Leonardo da Vinci had the right idea when he said, "I have offended God and mankind because my work didn't reach the quality it should have". Abraham Lincoln, steeped as he was in Christian sentiments, lived by the maxim, "We should be too big to take offense, and to noble to give it." For Rene Descartes, "Whenever anyone has offended me, I try to raise my soul so high that the offense cannot reach it."

Socrates held that it is better to suffer an injustice than to commit one. By the same token, it is better to be offended by another than to commit the same offense. The person whose principal interest in life is to avoid ever being offended will find that he has succeeded only in avoiding life. This was the tragic fate of T. S. Eliot's "J. Alfred Prufrock" who, in being excessively concerned about what other people were saying about him, became anxiety-ridden about "disturbing the universe" and finally ended his life by drowning. No one has the right to go through life without ever being offended. But we all have the obligation to do good and refrain from offending God.

OUR DUTY TO
THOSE IN NEED

The parable of the Good Samaritan stands as an inspirational example of helping those in need. The Good Samaritan may not have had a *duty*, strictly speaking, to come to the aid of the injured man who was left by the side of the road. No doubt he acted out of love. The Gospel commands us to love our neighbor. To what extent, we may ask, does the law require us to help another who is in distress? Under what circumstances does the law deem it our duty to come to the aid of a fellow human being? An example from the annals of law sheds an important light on the duty we have toward our neighbor.

In 1907, Orlando Dupue, a cattle buyer, was called to inspect cattle that were for sale at the home of Monsieur Flatau. It was a cold January night in Minnesota and Flatau invited the buyer to dine with him at his home. During the dinner, Depue was overcome by a "fainting spell," and became very weak and seriously ill. He asked permission to stay overnight, but was refused. Flatau led Depue out to his guest's sleigh, put him into it, adjusted the robes around him, and threw the reins, which he was too weak to hold, over his shoulders. Flatau then started the horses on the road to town. Depue was found the next morning by the side of the road and three-quarters of a mile away from the town. He was badly frost-bitten and nearly frozen to death. Depue sued.

The judge, imposing liability on Flatau for the loss of Depue's frostbitten fingers, stated: "In the case at bar defendants were under no contract obligation to minister to plaintiff in his distress; but humanity demanded they do so, if they understood and appreciated his condition . . . The law as well as humanity required that he {Depue} not be exposed in his helpless condition to the merciless elements" (*Depue v. Flatau* 100 Minn. 299, 111 N.W. 1, 1907). And so, the court ruled that the defendant owed Depue a *duty* upon discovering that he had been taken severely ill, not to expose him to danger on a cold winter night by sending him away unattended while he was in a fainting and helpless condition.

It is interesting to note that the court cited "humanity" as a compelling reason to help another in distress as exemplified in the Flatau/Depue case. It is not the written law, codified, studied, and cited, that defines the fundamental duties we have toward our neighbor. There is a higher law, a law of humanity that is sufficiently evident as not to require codification.

The Depue/Flatau case has been cited in an approving fashion by legal authorities and many subsequent court decisions. In one example, *The American Law Institute*, speaking in general, has stated that it makes no difference whether the helpless person is a guest or trespassed. He has the privilege of staying. His host has the duty not to injure or put him into an environment where he becomes nonviolable. The obligation arises when one person "understands and appreciates" the condition of the other (American Law Institute, *Restatement of Torts, Second* (1965) sec, 197).

A six-year-old boy was injured falling down an escalator. Store personnel, though they had time to stop the escalator before the child was hurt, failed to do so. The court cited the Depau/ Flatau case, stating, "Similarly, there is a duty to assist an invitee or business guest in time of peril, even though the initial injury was not caused by defendant's negligence. In the instant case, the store had the exclusive means of stopping the escalator and extricating the plaintiff." ("Negligent Failure to Stop Escalator," *Indiana Law Journal*: Vol. 17: Iss. 3, Article 7, 1942).

The pro-choice argument persists that a pregnant woman has no duty toward her unborn child. Abortion, in most instances, renders the unborn child "nonviable". This argument is not only dangerous for the unborn who are unwanted, but for everyone. If the principle prevails that no one has a duty toward anyone else, especially those in distress or need, then we are all doomed There is no place for the Good Samaritan in the pro-abortion handbook. A world of rights without duties is inimical to the law of "humanity". It needs to be reiterated that society is not held together by "contracts," but by love.

THE BACH TO SCHOOL PROGRAM

"Musick," wrote William Congreve in *The Mourning Bride*, "has Charms to sooth a savage Breast, To soften Rocks, or bend a knotted Oak". Congreve's words are far truer than he may have suspected, back in 1697. Music's healing effects have been well documented in contemporary clinical studies, although Congreve's reference to rocks and trees may be taken as poetic hyperbole.

Nonetheless, music's basic charms and healing potentialities have been recognized throughout history. Pythagoras called music, medicine. For Plato, "Music is a moral law. It gives soul to the universe, wings to the mind, flight to the imagination, and charm and gaiety to life and to everything." In the Middle Ages the study of music was a mandatory part of a physician's education.

One of the most dramatic accounts of the healing power of music is reported by William Styron. In his autobiography, *"Darkness Visible*: *A Memoir of Madness*, the celebrated novelist describes how music saved him from suicide. On listening to Brahms' *Alto Rhapsody* on the soundtrack of *The Bostonians*, he sensed that it brought back "all the joys the house had known . . . All this I realized was more than I could ever abandon . . . And just as powerfully I realized I could not commit this desecration on myself." Existentialist philosopher Gabriel Marcel claims that the music of Bach helped lead him into the Catholic Church. There are now more than 5,000 certified music therapists in the U.S.. More than 70 American colleges and universities offer music-therapy programs, treating a variety of conditions from posttraumatic stress disorder to Parkinson's disease, Alzheimer's and pain.

The world of music offers its own example of the healing power of music and how good can triumph over evil. In Modest Mussorgsky's *Night on Bald Mountain*, the distant ringing of the village church bell, the emergence of monks to pray matins, a beautiful and plaintive melody, together with the rising of the sun, all conspire to send the evil spirits back to the underworld. The effect is like holding up a crucifix to the face of Dracula.

Mussorgsky's masterpiece holds key to how goodness can disperse evil, a tactic that is now being discussed by the trustees of Toronto's Catholic schools. The board staff is presently considering the feasibility of piping Bach, Beethoven, and Mozart into school trouble zones. The tactic has worked in a number of cities where classical music is broadcast through PA systems in subways, malls, and train stations as a loitering deterrent and to disperse gangs. According to one report, "Whether it's Handel piped into New York's Port Authority or Tchaikovsky at a public library in London, the sound of classical music is apparently so repellent to teenagers that it sends them scurrying away like frightened mice." Private institutions such as McDonald's and 7-Eleven as well as countless shopping malls throughout the world have found the tactic to be a useful way of dispersing potentially troublesome youths

If music has charms to soothe the savage breast, what can be said for those who flee from the sound of the very best of music? It is a sad commentary on our present culture that a fine art, such as classical music can be employed as a kind of insect spray. Education, as Plato said long ago, should help people to love what is good and disdain what is bad. Something is seriously amiss when so many young people find classical music repellent and heavy rock addictive. What other inversions of the moral order does this phenomenon suggest!

How is healing possible when the very healing remedies proposed are deemed harmful? Back to Bach also suggests back to the basics. We have a natural appetite for what is good. That is the appetite that should be cultivated, not the appetite for thrills, power, and instant gratification. And back to basics means back to who we are as human beings and how our natural inclination to what is good is at the core of our being. Fleeing from the sound of classical music, then, is akin to fleeing from one's self. We also find this problem in the area of religion and philosophy which, though opportunities for education, become occasions for evacuation.

DEMOCRACY AND DESPOTISM

Alexis de Tocqueville's *Democracy in America* was recognized from the first as a political treatise of the first order. It
remains today, according to scholars of American history, as the
most perceptive and penetrating work of its kind. The author does
not idealize democracy. His intention was to show "to those who
have fancied an ideal democracy" that "they had clothed the picture in false colors." He does not hesitate to show, although he
is not opposed to democracy as such, how democracy in America
contains flaws that could lead to despotism.

He begins Volume II of his classic study with words that are
at least as true today as they were in 1835 when he penned them:
"I think that in no country in the civilized world is less attention
paid to philosophy than in the United States." Americans, then,
according to de Tocqueville, find "no need of drawing philosophical method out of books; they have found it in themselves." In
this regard, they unwittingly personify the isolationist thought of
Rene Descartes. "I think, therefore, I am" becomes "I think and
that's all that matters". Paradoxically, "America is therefore one
of the countries where the precepts of Descartes are least studied
and are best applied."

What this means for de Tocqueville is that because Americans are confined to their own thoughts, they become closed to the universal truths that form the content of true philosophy. Love of wisdom is directed toward universal truths, not the ethical relativism of private thoughts. This is a most serious deficiency, and de Tocqueville's trenchant observation appears now as a stunning prophesy: "Thus they [Americans] fall to denying what they cannot comprehend; which leaves them but little faith for whatever is extraordinary and an almost insurmountable distaste for whatever is supernatural." Consequently, "Each man thus retreats into himself from where he claims to judge the world."

This "distaste for whatever is supernatural" is now apparent on many fronts. Without a healthy regard for supernatural verities, America becomes immersed in the material and the practical, losing sight of the basis for the dignity of man, the importance of philosophy, the reality of God, the need for religion, the distinction between the sexes, the sacredness of marriage, and the splendor of truth. In their place, we have a pandemic of abortion and pornography, widespread atheism, the acceptance of same-sex marriage, and the promotion of euthanasia and anti-Christian attitudes.

There is a thread of self-reliance and independence that runs from what de Toqueville observed to what is transpiring in the present regime. Despite pockets of sectarian groups, such as the Puritans, Amish, Quakers, and so on, 19th century Americans saw democracy, by and large, in terms of moral and philosophical self-reliance, consistent with Ralph Waldo Emerson's paeans to this virtue ("Man is his own star"; "Trust thyself; every heart vibrates to that iron string").

People who flatter themselves as being "liberal" in today's society reduce moral values to something that is peculiarly their own. Thus, the widespread reluctance exists to "impose" one's own values, as if moral values were private and not universal. Abortion is permitted, to take but one example, because the commandment, "Thou shall not kill" is deemed much too supernatural to be comprehended. By logical extension, it is like saying, "I am personally opposed to war, but I do not want to impose my private values of peace on anyone." In the domain of theology, *dissent* is commonly interpreted as an expression of a free mind that will not be subordinated to any higher authority. But the absence of a genuine authority or reliable guide inevitably leads to chaos.

In this encyclical, *Veritatis Splendor,* John Paul II calls attention to the "*risk of an alliance between democracy and ethical relativism*" (sec. 101, emphasis his). He reasons that ethical relativism would "remove any sure moral reference point from political and social life, and on a deeper level make the acknowledgement of truth impossible." Without the guidance that real, objective values provide, ideas can easily be manipulated by those in power. "As history demonstrates," John Paul goes on to state, "a democracy without values easily turns into open or thinly disguised totalitarianism." Democracy is not self-correcting. If it is infected by ethical relativism, it can lead to the kind of despotism that de Tocqueville feared.

In 1993, John Paul II offered confirmation to what de Tocqueville observed more than 150 years ago as a weakness in democracy. This is a powerful testimony to the enduring value of philosophy. Philosophy is not "mine" but "ours". A nation flourishes when it embraces values it can share, not when it adopts an assortment of private views that bring about conflict, disharmony, and despotism.

TRANSCENDING ADVERSITY:
A MODERN JOB

The foregoing is an imagined dialogue between God and Satan. All the historical references pertaining to the musician, however, are true.

Satan: I understand that you are going to create a musician of extraordinary ability.

God: Yes, and I have done this many times before.

S: I hate music, especially music of soaring beauty. It reminds me too much of You.

G: Many philosophers and artists have correctly noted that "Beauty will save the world".

S: You were lucky with Beethoven. I did everything I could to prevent him from composing: an alcoholic father with a mean temper, a tubercular mother, penury, deafness.

G: Beethoven transcended adversity and his music brought much hope to millions of people.

S: But You did not succeed with Vladimir Lenin. He confessed, "I know nothing that is greater than [Beethoven's] *Appassionata*. It is marvelous superhuman music. I always think with pride—perhaps this is naïve of me—what marvelous things human beings can do."

G: "Superhuman" is the right word.

S: Lenin went on to say, "But I can't listen to music too often . . .makes me want to pat the heads of people . . . But now one must not pat anyone's head . . . one has to beat their heads, beat mercilessly . . . Hmm – it's a devilishly difficult task."

G: His reference to the devil is most appropriate. And what happened to Lenin?

S: Well, I am not my brother's keeper, but in his 54th year, he was murdered by poisoning at the hands of Stalin.

G: He who lives by the sword dies by the sword.

S: You need not remind me of that tired maxim; my business, however you want to ridicule it is still my business.

G: But a business that is not profitable for your victims.

S: Job and Beethoven kept the faith. I will see to it that your new creation will not.

G: He will succeed, despite your diabolical efforts.

S: I will send diphtheria into his life when he is 3 years old that will leave him blind for the rest of his life.

G: His parents will send him to a school for blind children and he will learn Braille. Eventually, he will compose in Braille. He will express gratitude for his blindness and tell people that it led him to music.

S: His birth will coincide with the outbreak of the Spanish Civil War.

G: I will arrange that his musical education will continue in Paris at the onset of the war.

S: Then I will persecute him when World War II commences. He will marry a woman who is Jewish.

G: I will see to his safe conduct out of Germany into Switzerland and back home to his native Spain. His wife will be a source of great personal support and professional assistance for him. She will be an outstanding pianist. Her name will be "Victoria".

S: Why does that have to be her name!

G: Because of what it presages.

S: All right! Now the *coup d'état*. His first child will die during childbirth.

G: He will grieve deeply over this loss, but it will inspire his greatest work, the *Adagio* of his *Concierto de Aranquez*, for guitar and orchestra. He will have another child, Cecilia, who will dedicate herself to promoting his music.

S: But, given all his trials, obstacles, and misfortunes, surely this will be a minor work and soon forgotten.

G: In the words of one esteemed musicologist, this work "has become, quite simply, the most successful concerto written for any instrument in this century".

S: You are referring to the 20th Century. That was supposed to be *my* century! I chose this century to do my worst against You.

G: You said this to Pope Leo XIII in his vision of you, a truly horrifying vision which prompted him to write the Prayer to St. Michael the Archangel. This prayer was then said throughout the world at the end of every Mass.

S: I wanted him to despair, as I wanted your new creation.

G: Joachín Rodrigo lived from 1901 to 1999. He is the "tranquil flower" on the "tortured stem," offering the world a transcendent hope that soars above all the pain, grief, and disillusionment that plagued the 20th century. He is the anti-Satan of your century. Satan, you cannot defeat Me!

—PART SEVEN—
LIFE AND SEXUALITY

"Mankind declares this with one deafening voice: that sex may be ecstatic so long as it's also restricted. This is the beginning of all purity; and purity is the beginning of all passion."
– G. K. Chesterton

The Disappearance of Nature

Prof. Lewis Samuel Feuer informed the readers of *The New York Times Magazine* in 1966 that "American philosophy is dead". He did acknowledge that it lingered on in a surrogate form, but was drowning in a sea of words that no longer connected with reality. He expressed his doubts as to whether such academic stalwarts as William James, Sigmund Freud, John Dewey, or Albert Einstein would be able to obtain a Ph. D. in any of the country's philosophy departments because their ideas would not pass the language test of formal logic. Considering how philosophy has remained moribund over the past half-century, Feuer's contention was both accurate and prophetic.

Philosophers are uniquely self-destructive creatures insofar as they allow themselves to be intimidated by one of philosophy's proper objects – nature. Einstein's advice to "Look deep into nature, and then you will understand everything better" has been replaced by "isolate yourself from nature and be content to analyze words". As a result, modern philosophy in America offers little to help man understand himself, his surroundings, and the meaning of life. In the absence of nature there is not much for the philosopher to sink his teeth into. Philosophy becomes purely abstract, although nature stubbornly continues to exist.

Philosophy, in its authentic mode, is crucial in clarifying the link between law and justice. It sheds light on who we are as human beings and how we should live. It illuminates, in fact, the path to wisdom. We discard philosophy at our own peril. Yet, despite its importance, it is rejected for something that ill serves the public interest.

George F. Will put his finger on the problem in his 1983 book, *Statecraft as Soulcraft*. "Modern political philosophy," he wrote, "has transformed a fact (man's appetitive nature) into a moral principle." This means that "Man should be allowed, even encouraged, to do what he most desires to do." Given modern man's propensity for sexual indulgence, he has elevated a carnal desire to a civic right. The notion of unnatural desires is no longer relevant because nature is no longer relevant. Naked desire can hardly serve as the underpinning for a healthy society. For Prof. Will, "A nation--a civilization--so constituted cannot long endure."

The cities of Boston, Washington, and San Francisco, and the state of Illinois now regard Catholic Charities as an organization that is unfit to place children for adoption. Their unacceptable flaw is that they want what is best for the adoptees and they believe that placing children in same-sex marriages is not in their best interest. But if the realities of husband, wife, and marriage are not grounded in nature, Catholic Charities has no just claim for its position. Same-sex marriages, together with the right of the partners to adopt children, take primacy over traditional marriages because they are based on a desire. As a consequence, Catholic Charities is viewed as discriminatory because it does not regard all forms of marriage as equal. Thus, Catholic Charities is no longer free to be itself and to continue to serve the public generously as it has done over a long period of time.

Speaking out against this deprivation of religious freedom, Cardinal Francis George laments that, "Our vaunted American liberties" are "all being traded off in favor of freedom of sexual expression." This is a most disturbing trend because the danger now exists that all Catholic charitable institutions will eventually be replaced by government agencies that are not primarily concerned about public welfare, but about imposing the ideological acceptance of an array of sexual desires, some of which are clearly contrary to nature.

Is it discriminatory for a fire department not to hire someone who is a pyromaniac, or for a bank not to hire a kleptomaniac? In these instances, there would be no discrimination against the person, but a prudent judgment that takes into consideration the characteristic actions of these candidates. The Church does not discriminate against persons, holding that all human being are created in the image of God, but She does exercise the right to make judgments about whether certain acts (which may lead to death, for example) are contrary to nature and not good for human beings. The Church is being attacked for being reasonable and trying to help people in a realistic way.

In attempting to eradicate discrimination, America has now set in motion the very worst kind of discrimination -- penalizing people and institutions for trying to help others on a realistic basis. Nature will not go away; She will be triumphant in the end (but at what price!).

DECONSTRUCTION AND

THE INCARNATION

The word "deconstruction," very much like the word "existentialism," has a certain cachet. It enjoys currency among those who want to be "hip to what is hip". It presumes to be a legitimate branch of philosophy, but its trendiness and superficiality are hardly consistent with philosophy as the perennial search for wisdom. It is fashionable among university intellectuals who pride themselves for being *avant garde*. For those outside of academe, "deconstruction" is regarded as a synonym for gobbledygook.

The deconstructionist begins by doubting the firm reality of just about everything. As a result, he comes to believe that certain verities that people have long taken for granted, such as morality, religion, nature, and art, have all been arbitrarily constructed and therefore need to be de-constructed. Very little remains once these verities have all be deconstructed or "erased," to employ a favorite word of many deconstructionists. There appears to be very little that is not susceptible to being deconstructed. One writer contends that "the laws of physics are merely social conventions, like traffic laws."

Deconstruction, therefore, is a process that opens up a vast area of freedom. Once reality has been deconstructed, individuals are pretty much free to be or to do whatever they please. Here,

Jean-Paul Sartre's famous dictum comes into play: "existence precedes essence". But the road to this wide open freedom is also the road to nihilism, though some deconstructionists attest that it is "nihilism with a happy ending". Nonetheless, the notion of unbounded freedom has appeal for many people. Realistically, however, if we have nothing to stand on, we remain unable to move.

One important area of deconstruction is gender. Traditionally, gender has always been closely associated with male and female and its most authoritative pronouncement is in the *Book of Genesis* where God states, "Male and female he created them". But now, under the knife of deconstruction, "gender" is regarded as an arbitrary construct. As a result, gender becomes something that one chooses. University Professor, Judith Butler offers the following explanation: "When the constructed status of gender is theorized as radically independent of sex, gender itself becomes a free-floating artifice, with the consequence that man and masculine might just as easily signify a female body as a male one, and woman and feminine a male body as easily as a female one" (*Gender Trouble*: *Feminism and the Subversion of Identity*).

The social media offers popular images of celebrities who seem to personify what Dr. Butler is saying. Consider the protean images portrayed by the likes of Boy George, Mick Jagger, Madonna, Eddie Izzard, Marilyn Manson, Lady Gaga, and various drag queens. Once gender is deconstructed, anything goes, except, of course, holding to the notion that sex and gender are intrinsic to the human being and provide a reliable basis for the Natural Law.

Butler is one a number of feminists who have deconstructed womanhood itself. Julia Kristeva, for example, maintains that "Strictly speaking, 'women' cannot be said to exist." She argues that although there are no women (because that would constitute a stereotype), we should keep using the term because it represents political advantages for women. Such radical feminists are not afraid of indulging in contradictions. Nonetheless, more logically minded feminists, insist that if there is one reality that feminists must uphold, it is the reality of the feminine. Christina Hoff Sommers, a feminist in her own right, has authored a book appropriately titled, *Who Stole Feminism*?

Nature is a stubborn reality and will not be banished by an academic trend. As Cicero said, long ago, "Custom will never conquer nature; nature will always remain unconquerable" (*Numquam naturam mos vinceret; est enim semper invicta*"). For Christians, the Incarnation of Christ, the Word made Flesh, is a definitive indication of the reality of the body, as well as the reality of sex and gender. It is a small wonder, then, that deconstructionists regard the *logos*, personified in the Gospel according to St. John, as "the enemy". The Incarnation of Christ as definitively a man is an article of faith. But the reality of nature and gender are also validated by simple observation and common sense. One's gender is usually the first thing we notice in another person and the last thing we are likely to forget.

GENDER IN 50
DIFFERENT FLAVORS

It has been long thought that there were just two sexes. After all, *Genesis* proclaimed that God created them "male" and "female". All cultures throughout history have seen fit to distinguish the sexes in this manner. There are separate restrooms and separate Olympic events for men and for women. Men and women are distinctive in their attire, their voices, and in their biology. When a baby comes into the world, the first question is whether it is a boy or a girl. Tax forms require a check in the boxes marked "m" or "f". The sex of a person, male or female, is the first thing you notice in another and the last thing you are likely to forget. How important is the binary division of the sexes to society? According to sociologist Margaret Mead, "If any human society—large or small, simple or complex, based on the most rudimentary hunting and fishing, or on the whole elaborate interchange of manufactured products—is to survive, it must have a pattern of social life that comes to terms with the differences between the sexes."

Well, as a result of a revolution of staggering proportions, all this has changed. Facebook, the social media giant that serves approximately 1.15 billion monthly users throughout the world, is adding 50 different terms by which people can identify their sexuality. Among the new sexual identities are "androgynous," "bi-gender," "intersex," "gender fluid," and "transsexual". However, this may be too limiting a number for those who see gender as a spectrum that may contain an infinite number of sexual identities.

How has this come about and is it something which we must all come to accept? Its roots are in a form of Neo-Marxism that sees the relationship between man and woman not as complementary, but as oppressive. Just as, according to Marx, the capitalist class oppresses the working class, men oppress women. In the words of Friedrich Engels, "The first class antagonism in history coincides with the antagonism between men and women in monogamous marriage, and the first class oppression with that of the female sex by the male."

The revolution that Marx and Engels initiated was liberation from oppression so that each individual would gain the freedom to become himself/herself. The oppressed class was a stereotype. Gender feminists, following Marxism, have sought to eradicate three categories of stereotypes by deconstructing masculinity and femininity, mother, father, husband, and wife, and finally, socially constructed roles that are assigned to one sex or the other. Thus, the deconstructionist philosopher Jacques Lacan can proclaim, "There is no such thing as Woman."

Once liberated from stereotypes and artificial categories, people would no longer feel trapped. Because gender, according to the theory, was entirely socially constructed, people could define themselves as they pleased. In a paper prepared for the Beijing Conference on Women, Anne Fausto Sterling penned, "The Five Sexes: Why Male and Female Are Not Enough." She added "herms," merms," and "ferms" to the traditional two. *First Things* reported that the University of Chicago was adding new bathrooms for those who felt uncomfortable about classifying themselves within the "hegemonic taxonomies of bourgeois hetero-normativity".

Jean-Paul Sartre, a Marxist in his own right, went as far as to state that there is no such thing as a human being. He did not want the person whom convention refers to as a human being to be imprisoned by a label. His philosophy called for "absolute freedom". Simone de Beauvoir, the long-time colleague of Sartre, begins her epoch-making book, *The Second Sex*, by declaring that the term "female" is derogatory "because it imprisons her in her sex". For Sartre and de Beauvoir, "existence precedes essence".

The current fascination with a multiplicity of genders is based on two erroneous assumptions. The first is that all men oppress all women. All the loving marriages throughout history, and they are numberless, attest to this fallacy. The second is that freedom reaches its zenith in the absence of any restricting nature. One misguided thinker believed that a bird could fly at maximum speed if it flew in a resistance-less vacuum. In a vacuum, of course, the bird could not breathe nor would it have any air against which it could flap its wings.

The fact that one is a woman does not restrict her identity as an individual person. As Shakespeare says of Cleopatra, "Age cannot wither her, nor custom stale her infinite variety" (*Antony and Cleopatra*). Our nature does not limit us, but defines us. Our truest freedom is not in becoming something we cannot be, but in being ourselves, something that requires both freedom and realistic common sense.

WHERE HAVE ALL THE
BOYS AND GIRLS GONE?

It has been a virtual global and historical axiom that gender is rooted in sex, that masculine and feminine have their respective bases in male and female. Sex is biological, gender, although very much rooted in biology, is influenced by culture. What has been taken as axiomatic, however, is now undergoing deconstruction. The new view that is gaining headway is that gender is entirely constructed by society and therefore should be liberated from nature so that individuals can choose their own gender.

Thus, Anne Fausto Sterling presented a paper at the Beijing Conference on Women entitled, "The Five Sexes: Why Male and Female Are Not Enough". She added "herms," "merms," and "ferms" to the traditional two. Others envision far more than five genders. Deconstructionist philosopher Jacques Lacan, along with the support of similar thinking feminists, has declared, "There is no such thing as Woman".

The practical implications of this revolution are being felt, especially in universities. *First Things* reported that the University of Chicago was adding new bathrooms for those who feel uncomfortable about classifying themselves within what is called, the "hegemonic taxonomies of bourgeois heteronormativity". Translation: the middle class im-position of a two-sex classification.

Here is an instance of what David Leyman, in his excellent cri-
tique of de-construction (*Signs of the Times*) refers to as de-construction's "idiosyncratic and arcane vocabulary".

Wendy Shalit, author of *A Return to Modesty*, reports from
Williams College that at the beginning of each year, male and female students in each dormitory unit vote on whether or not to
have coed bathrooms. The vote always goes for coed bathrooms
because those who might vote for privacy are intimidated by the
charge that they are not comfortable with their bodies. Nonetheless, in this awkward and inviting situation, males are sternly
warned against objectifying women with their "male gaze". The
first step is to invite mayhem, the second step is to condemn it
when it occurs.

The Lincoln Public School District in Nebraska has decided,
contrary to parental approval, to implement a free-wheeling gender program. They are told not to address children as "boys and
girls" and not to separate them into lines or groups that are based
on the traditional "heteronormative" model. Students are encouraged to choose their own self-identifying pronouns. A boy may
prefer to be called "she," while a girl may prefer to be called "he".
Or they might prefer altogether different pronouns. This is all done
in the interest of getting the children to "think more expansively".
Parents, who have not yet undergone any deconstruction of their
own sexual identities, have complained about what they regard as
a sinister form of indoctrination imposed on their children.

"Thinking more expansively," however, may carry the price
of not thinking essentially. The gender of another is the first thing
we notice and the last thing we are likely to forget. It is entrenched
in all those many languages that employ gender terms prior nouns
and pronouns. Will the new generation prefer listening to *Il Tra-
viata* and *La Trovotore*? Can languages by expunged from their
gender terms? Can history, as well as all literature, be re-written
so that the terms "boys" and "girls" do not trap people in atavistic

stereotypes? Will Maurice Chevalier's rendition of "Thank heaven for little girls" be placed on an index of forbidden songs? What will replace the maxim, "boys will be boys"?

Nature is that fundamental reality that will not allow itself to be deconstructed. Education must build on nature just as what we eat must conform to the biological nature of the digestive system. The attempt to deconstruct nature is at the same time, the attempt to destroy it, which is a rather futile endeavor. As Steven Goldberg states in the *Inevitability of Patriarchy*, "it is terribly self-destructive to refuse to accept one's own nature and the joys and powers it invests." In this light, Cicero is worth quoting, "Custom will never conquer nature; for nature always remains unconquerable" (*Numquam naturam mos vinceret; est enim ea semper invicta*).

WHEN IS BULLYING
PERMISSIBLE?

He is now a journalist, but he remembers, with painful clarity, a learning experience he had when in Grade 7. He had made the politically incorrect act of writing the word "fireman". His teacher, an apostle of gender-free nouns and "inclusive" language, slashed a big red X across the offending word and replaced it with "firefighter". "The severity of that slash," he recalls, "thick and bleeding with disapproval--was mortifying because, even as a kid, I recall thinking that my teacher thought I was sexist."

Can we categorize the teacher's action as bullying? There are four types of bullying: physical, verbal, emotional, and cyber. Emotional bullying occurs, according to one authority, when "one partner might make statements in such a manner as to bring about distress to the other partner." It would seem, then, that the teacher's action renders her guilty of bullying, though she may very well have regarded her action as pedagogical and in the interest of bringing about a better world. What liberties may be taken in the interest of indoctrinating students into an ideology? Can a feminist teacher ever be indicted as a bully? Or do they have diplomatic immunity?

What, we may ask, did our 7th grade student learn from this experience? He "learned" (or feared) that he was "sexist" and was

DR. DONALD DEMARCO

left wondering how serious this label might be. The red X was more guilt-imposing than educational. If he had only misspelled the word "fireman," his reprisal would have been much kinder. Indoctrinating political correctness, it appears, at least in this case, takes precedence over teaching the three Rs: reading, 'riting and 'rithmetic. Political correctness does not abide patience.

The alleged invidiousness of so-called "exclusive language" is stated by feminist author Marie Shearer: "Sexist language is no less noxious than racist language. As Kett and Underwood say in their recent book, "Avoiding *he* is equal to taking down the 'whites only' sign in a restaurant." Yet, this is sheer exaggeration. More importantly, however, it is inflammatory. The use of generic pronouns is consistent with Standard English, as attested by the dictionary. Women have no reason to feel excluded when they hear such expressions as "all men are created equal," "he who hesitates is lost," "no man is an island," "danger – man-eating sharks," or "he who laughs last, laughs best"? The bullying techniques of the inclusive language brigade is, according to sociologist Peter Berger, offensive. Inclusive language, he writes, "is an ideological jargon whose purpose is to compel allegiance in a symbolic fashion. This is why I find it offensive."

What happens when the immovable object meets the irresistible force, which is to say, when the opponents of exclusivity clash with the opponents of offensiveness? What happens when the opponents of bullying clash with another group that opposes bullying? It is political correctness on a collision course with itself. On the other hand, why not simply speak English and honor the meaning of words. "All men are created equal" is inclusive, extending to men as well as women.

Garson Kanin's celebrated play, *Born Yesterday*, is about the empowerment through education of a not-so-dumb blonde. In her crash course, Billie Dawn inquires about the meaning of Alexander Pope's famous phrase, "The proper study of Mankind is Man".

141

"Of course, that means women, too," she says, rather offhandedly. When Billie is assured that it does, the diligent student indicates that she knew it all the time: "Yes, I know." There was no need for further discussion in this 1945 comedy. Billie could be educated without becoming a hard line feminist. She knew that Mankind included women and excluded animals.

Every word includes what it means and excludes its contradictories. "Book" includes books and excludes non-books, just as "woman" includes woman and excludes non-women. Bullying has no place in education, nor do approaches to learning which are clearly offensive. Let a married couple, Peter and Brigitte Berger, both sociologists, have the last word: "Femspeak," they write, "must be understood as part of the cultural imperialism of the new knowledge class, seeking to impose its language, values, and political control over other classes in the society . . . a linguistic offensive that is part of a general political strategy."

—PART EIGHT—
LIFE AND MARRIAGE

"The Christian religion, by confining marriage to pairs, and rendering the relation indissoluble, has by these two things done more toward the peace, happiness, settlement, and civilization of the world, than by any other part in this whole scheme of divine wisdom."
– Edmund Burke

THE NATURALNESS OF MARRIAGE

"The friendship between man and wife," wrote Aristotle in his *Nichomachean Ethics*, "seems inherently in us by nature. For man is by nature more inclined to live in couples than to live as a social and political being." The essential point he is making here, which is in danger of being lost in the modern world, is that marriage is fundamentally *natural* rather than *political*. In his *Politics*, the Stagirite reinforces this statement when he states that "man is an animal more inclined by nature to connubial than political society".

Aristotle was a meticulous student of nature. And as a philosopher, he knew how to place things in their proper order. He understood, therefore, that marriage, with its personal satisfactions, its intimacy, its security, and its potential for generating offspring, is naturally superior to the more tenuous and far less personal relationships that are political and social. For much of the same reasons, Aquinas could state that the best of all friendships is that between husband and wife.

In reviewing the high suicide rates of single men throughout Europe in the nineteenth century, Emile Durkhein reasoned that "the bond attaching the [single] man to life relaxes because that attaching him to society is itself slack." Common experience should be enough to convince us that the bond of matrimony is far more secure and durable than any relationship one might have between himself and society. Marriage is natural, whereas political arrangements are conventional. Therefore, marriage has a built-in inclination toward personal fulfillment that is both original and universal.

A critical question, however, remains. Why is it that marriage, rooted in nature as it is, so often ends in failure? St. Thomas Aquinas was concerned about this question in the thirteenth century. He reasoned that "nature" means two things. In the first instance, it refers to a necessary connection between the natural thing and its end. Aquinas uses the simple example of fire moving upwards. Fire cannot help doing anything other than moving in this particular direction. It is compelled by nature to do so.

Marriage relates to "nature" in the second meaning. In this case, what is natural does not achieve its end of necessity. Marriage provides a basis and an inclination, but will not achieve its end without the husband and wife nourishing its development with love and care. To put the matter more concretely, marriage demands the ceaseless application of virtue and intelligence in order to meet the unpredictable challenges that life and society present. A vessel may be seaworthy, but will not reach its destination unless it is steered in the right direction. Marriage, despite its naturalness, is no guarantee of happiness. It must be cultivated, a task that, at times, can be most demanding. The Church is wise in understanding that marriage is a sacrament that can be nourished by God Himself. No political arrangement has ever been regarded as sacramental.

"And they lived happily ever after," does not apply to marriage. No one would deny its difficulties, restrictions, and inconveniences. Yet, these pale in comparison with the great benefits that marriage and the family confer. The great poet Johann Wolfgang von Goethe put marriage in the proper perspective when he wrote the following: "Marriage is the beginning and summit of civilization. It tames the brute, and even the most civilized one has no better opportunity to prove that he is civilized. Marriage must be indissoluble; for it brings so much happiness that any unhappiness here or there is completely outweighed by that."

Goethe certainly recognized the share of inconveniences that marriage brings: "It may at times be inconvenient, this I can well believe—and this should be so. Aren't we also married to our consciences which we often would gladly get rid of, because it is much more inconvenient than any husband or wife could ever be?"

If marriage fails, it is not because it lacks a natural basis. Rather, when it fails, it does so because it is not nurtured. Nature is what the spouses are given. The nurturing is up to them. It is easy to sentimentalize marriage. But it is also easy to trivialize it. It is sentimentalized when nurture is disregarded. It is trivialized when it is uprooted from nature and treated as a mere contract. Marriage remains, however, a synthesis of bedrock nature and firm commitment.

MARRIAGE AND MARKETING

Some years ago there were two companies that produced canned salmon. For one, the salmon was pink; for the other, it was white. Popular perception was that the pink was more natural and healthier than the white. As a result, consumers purchased the canned pink salmon in such relative proportions that they threatened to drive the white salmon manufacturers out of business. An ingenious marketing expert saved the day for his company by putting the following words on the label of the white salmon: "Guaranteed not to turn pink in the can". This clever ruse nearly drove the producers of pink salmon out of business. The case went to court, but not until the reputations of both varieties of canned salmon was restored.

Marketing is a strategy that can convince people of the merits of something without presenting them with any justifying information. People who smoked *Kools* swore that these cigarettes actually cooled their throats. They believed what it said on the label, and nothing more. This is the same problem that Socrates encountered in Plato's dialogue, *Gorgias*, in dealing with the sophists who held that they did not need to provide people with knowledge in order to persuade them about the merits of something. Socrates concluded that this form of persuasion could work only among the ignorant and only in a crowd.

If the Gadfly of Athens were alive today, he would still en-
counter people persuading others without providing them with the
requisite information that would justify their beliefs. Marketing
strategists have succeeded, to a significant extent, in convinc-
ing others that marriage should not be restricted to a man and a
,woman. These modern sophists do this by asserting, but without
substantiating, that same-sex marriage is a civil right. As a consequence, anyone who opposes same-sex marriage is said to be
against human rights and therefore unjust, unwelcoming, and un-
civil. These are most serious accusations and places those who
defend traditional marriage in somewhat of a quandary.

The assertion that same-sex marriage is a civil right, however, is specious. No one has the right to change the meaning of
marriage, one that has enjoyed universal approbation throughout
the world and throughout the course of history. If one did have this
right, he could just as well change marriage back to its traditional
form. The claim that anyone can change the definition of anything
by sheer will power would not be an effecting marketing tool. But
to associate same-sex marriage with civil rights, although purely a
marketing trick, has proved most effective.

President Obama delivered a commencement address on
June 14, 2014 and told the graduating class of the University of
California at Irvine, and all those in attendance, that same-sex
marriage is about marrying the person you love. A moment's reflection reveals that no one can possibly believe this. Can a mother
marry her beloved children? Can a married man marry any other
woman or man that he happens to love? The president's ruse is
sophistical. It is effective because it presupposes a mass audience
who are either ignorant or unthinking. Similarly, the Massachusetts Supreme Court ruled that "the right to marry means little if
it does not include the right to marry the person of one's choice".
The minimal condition for marriage—*mutual* consent—seems to

have but a subtlety that the judges of the Supreme Court of Massachusetts failed to recognize. Yet, this marketing trick made same-
sex marriage legal in the Bay State. The judges proved to be more
pernicious than judicious.

In a *Seinfeld* sitcom episode, George Costanza, who exhibited no acting skills whatsoever, insisted that his starting salary for
a pilot project should be commensurate with that of Ted Danson.
George's logic was something like this: If Ted Danson is an actor
and I am an actor, we should get the same salary. George simply
omitted the inconvenient but sizeable gap between the abilities of
the two. Similarly, advocates of same-sex marriage argue as follows: Since both heterosexuals and homosexuals want to marry,
they should be treated equally. These two arguments are equally
bogus because they omit what is most relevant and validating. In
the first example, it is acting ability; in the second example, it is
the complementarity that belongs to the very essence of marriage.

The dispute between the two companies that produced
canned salmon was settled in the court. The dispute between tradition marriage and same-sex marriage will finally be settled in the
court of public opinion. The critical question, however, is this: will
public opinion on this crucial issue be formed by knowledge and
careful reflection, or will it be formed by the unthinking masses?

A NEW WORD FOR THE FAMILY

Archbishop Vincenzo Paglia, president of the Pontifical Council for the Family, may have coined a new word when he described contemporary American society as "defamilied". While some participants in the Synod of Bishops may think that the Church should make things easier for Christian spouses, the archbishop contends that "We have to ask more of families".

His position is well taken. Contraception, sterilization, abortion, same-sex marriage, certain forms of reproductive technology, the negative birthrate, along with other divisive factors, have, according to Archbishop Paglia, caused the family to be "torn apart for the first time in history". The last thing that is needed is to weaken marriage and the family by capitulating even further to secular mores. An athlete, whose substandard performance is due to his being overweight, does not improve his performance by becoming even more overweight. The "defamilied" family must be "refamilied".

Currently, in America, 75% of youths grow up without fathers, while nearly 50% of adults live alone. Abortion is rampant, and contraception is taken for granted. The family has splintered. What is urgently needed is a return to the integrity of the family. The text book axiom that the family is the basic unit of society is now being replaced by the notion that the individual is the basic unit of society. Needless to say, the very meaning of society includes non-individualistic notions such as unity, cooperation, solidarity, and a common good. Sheer individualism breeds chaos, and chaos breeds violence.

The family is irreplaceable as the foundation of society. For G. K. Chesterton, "This triangle of truisms, of father, mother and child, cannot be destroyed: It can only destroy those civilizations which disregard it." It is, as Pope Benedict XVI has stated, "an intermediate institution between individuals and society, and nothing can completely take its place." The family, then, honors the uniqueness of each individual child, but, through love and proper education, assists and directs them toward their proper place in society. In other words, the family raises *persons* who are simultaneously unique individuals and responsible members of the community. There can be no real community without real persons.

Saint John Paul II has described the indispensable role of the family in the following terms: "The first and fundamental structure for 'human ecology' is the *family*, in which man receive his first formative ideas about truth and goodness, and learns what it means to love and be loved, and thus what it actually means to be a person." This is why the former Pontiff never tired of reiterating that the *person* is central to the development and maintenance of culture.

The great problem that bishops face now is how to make a true Christian family attractive in a culture that is more dedicated to individualism. This problem is akin to the more universal problem of how to make personal sacrifice appealing in a culture that is dominated by self-gratification. This is essentially the age-old problem of how to make Christianity plausible in an atmosphere where sin is prevalent.

Individuality alone is an illusion. One's moral strength, his ability to resist corrupting temptations is owed largely to the love and formation he received from his family. Theologian Stanley Hauerwas could not have said it better: "Without the family, and the inter-generational ties involved, we have no way to know what it means to be historic beings. As a result we become determined by rather than determining our histories. Set out in the world with no family, without a story of and for the self, we will simply be captured by the reigning ideologies of the day."

The increasingly loose structure that is now called a "family" needs to return to the original notion of a family, modeled by the Holy Family and honored throughout the generations and throughout the world. By strengthening the family, the individual as well as society become strengthened. The experiment of trying to replace the family with individualism has run its course and the unhappy results should be plain to see. Archbishop Paglia is on sold ground when he says that individualism is a "virus," and "The first victim of this virus is the family, the first place where everything begins."

THE END OF MOTHERHOOD

In May of 1971, an article by Edward Grossman appeared in *Atlantic* entitled, "The Obsolescent Mother". He predicted that the day would come when a woman's two laparoscopy scars will be as commonplace as our smallpox vaccination mark. At age twenty, every female will be superovulated and her eggs will be collected and frozen. This is a particular good age, according to the author, since at that youthful stage women are less likely to conceive a Down syndrome child or one that has other congenital defects.

Thereafter, whenever a woman wants to become a mother, she will simply have one of her eggs thawed, fertilized in a dish, and gestated in an artificial incubator. The uterus will become vestigial, though the ovaries will remain important. No woman will lose her figure due to childbearing. Grossman predicted that "women who wish to put up with the old style and all that it implies will be free to do so. But it will be a throwback and increasingly rare as the manifest advantages of the artificial womb make it likely to win the competition."

Now, in the year 2014, Grossman's predictions have not been quite fulfilled. Nonetheless, according to NBC News, mega-tech companies, Apple and Facebook have agreed to cover the cost of egg freezing for their female employees. Apparently, these two technology giants do not want to lose important female employee hours. Babies can always wait. Apart from the moral issues, which are sundry, has technology advanced to the state where egg freezing, thawing, and subsequent fertilization in a dish is feasible?

The Society for Assisted Reproductive Technology estimates that the chance of one frozen egg leading to a live birth for a woman of 38 years is 2-12 percent. This age is significant since the average age of a woman who elects egg freezing is 37.4. In 2011 fewer than ten babies worldwide were believed to have been born from eggs frozen from women 38 and older. After reading 112 articles relevant to the safety and efficacy of egg freezing, Samantha Pfeifer, representing the American Society for Reproductive Medicine, stated that, "Marketing this technology for the purpose of deferring childbearing may give women false hope."

The notion that there is a "competition," as Grossman called it, between a woman's procreative processes and technology is, itself, quite artificial. Can motherhood be segmented into separate parts? Or is motherhood best understood as a continuity that begins with the loving embrace and continues through conception, gestation, delivery, and lactation? Can various stages of motherhood be exteriorized without something important being lost in the process?

The artificial incubator, together with egg freezing and in vitro fertilization can exteriorize procreation completely. Can a woman be prepared for motherhood when motherhood is artificially prepared for her? Will they be able to cultivate maternal feelings or responsibilities for their children while those children are developing apart from them? What will become of maternal bonding? Will this augur the end of motherhood?

Marge Piercy's book, *Woman on the Edge of Time*, is considered a kind of bible for many feminists. Its central message is that only by giving up their power of reproduction can equality between the sexes be achieved. The price, of course, would be the end of motherhood. On a more humane note, sociologist Jean Bethke Elshtain maintains that the "core of *human* ethics requires "men and women to join together in opposing a headlong race toward social engineering." "Otherwise," she warns, "we will face more insidious political domination than we have ever known." Something may still be said for the "old style".

WHETHER INDUCED ABORTION IS AN INSTANCE OF DOMESTIC VIOLENCE (IN THE STYLE OF ST. THOMAS AQUINAS)

Objection 1. It seems that induced abortion is not an instance of domestic violence, but a *choice.* Since there is nothing inherent in a choice that would include violence, induced abortion cannot be an instance of violence. Moreover, it would seem to be an act of violence to prevent people from making their own choices.

Objection 2. The claim that induced abortion is an instance of domestic violence is political in nature and is used to attack a woman's constitutional right. Decisions of a moral nature should not be determined by politics.

Objection 3. Domestic violence refers to acts of violence involving people who are already born. Therefore, it does not apply to those who are still in the womb. A minute cell can hardly be regarded as a human being.

Objection 4. The real violence involved is the attack on the mother by an aggressive fetus. Abortion, therefore, *protects* women against violence.

On the contrary, Induced abortion, because it involves a forcible attack against a mother's unborn child is manifestly an act of domestic violence. In fact, it is an ultimate form of violence since it is, in almost every case, an act that destroys the life of the unborn child.

I answer that, The child in the womb is a human being and part of the human family. The forcible termination of his life is clearly an act of violence in a domestic setting. This is recognized even by those who approve abortion. Doctors Willard Gaylin and Marc Lappe, for example, recognize that in abortion the child is subjected to "unimaginable acts of violence" such as "dismemberment, salt-induced osmotic shock, or surgical extirpation." Furthermore, the mother of the child approves such acts. Hence, induced abortion is an act of domestic violence.

Reply Obj. 1. The term *choice* does not include that which is chosen. Morality hinges on the object of one's choice. A choice may be a good choice, for example, when it is a choice for life. On the other hand, may be an evil choice in the case of choosing to kill an innocent human being. Induced abortion, then, since it is opposed to innocent life, is an evil choice.

Reply Obj. 2. A law that protects an unjust act is not a law in the proper sense of the term. A just law must protect what is good and serve the common good. Since abortion is unjust to the unborn and robs them of their life, it is an unjust law and as such does not grant a woman a *right* to abort. A right must not be construed as doing anything one pleases, but doing what is right.

Reply Obj. 3. The sciences of biology and fetology make it clear that human life begins when sperm from the male fertilizes a female egg. The complete genetic code is present in the unborn child at this earliest stage. The single-cell *zygote* possesses all the genes and DNA that it will ever need as it advances toward being a 30-trillion cell adult. The unborn child is not a *potential* human being, but a human being with a great deal of potential.

Reply Obj. 4. The unborn child is involved in a developmental process that is natural for both him as well as for his mother. During the period of gestation, therefore, the child is not aggressing against its mother, but peacefully seeking its own development. Under normal circumstances the child in the womb confers benefits on the pregnant mother, including safeguarding her against certain diseases. The mother-child-in-the-womb relationship is natural and symbiotic, not predatory in any way.

—PART NINE—
LIFE AND GRATITUDE

"The so-called life not worth living does not exist."
– Viktor Frankl

GIVING THANKS

The word "thanks" is etymologically rooted in the word "thought". With this in mind, G. K. Chesterton could say: "I would maintain that thanks are the highest form of thought, and that gratitude is happiness doubled by wonder."

Chesterton had a genius for expressing expansive ideas in a concise way. Many of his phrases belong to the province of compressed wisdom. In life, we either take things for granted or we offer thanks. The factor that causes us to stop in our tracks when we think about something extraordinary is wonder. That very wonder that prompts us to think also confers upon us a certain happiness. It is indeed wonderful to be alive! To be filled with wonder is at the same time to be suffused with happiness. As a result, rather than simply taking things in stride, we respond with gratitude and enjoy the benefits of a higher world.

Furthermore, gratitude must be directed to a person. We say, quite casually, "thank goodness," or "thank heaven," or "thank your lucky stars". Yet these are not the factors to which we owe our thanks. Returning to the quotable G. K., "We thank people for birthday presents of cigars and slippers. Can I thank no one for the birthday present of birth?" How easy it is to miss the obvious, being distracted by the superfluous! "When we were children we were grateful to those who filled our stockings at Christmas time," the redoubtable Chesterton added, "why are we not grateful to God for filling our stockings with legs?" Shakespeare has Henry VI exclaim, "O Lord that lends me life, Lend me a heart replete with thankfulness." Gratitude is our heart's applause to God's generosity.

The very worst moment for the atheist is when he feels a compelling urge to be thankful, but has no one to thank. Thanks must be directed to a person because it is a person who is our benefactor. We thank God, and in so doing complement the Giver's gift with the receiver's gratitude.

But there is more to unlock in Chesterton's *bon mot*. Along with thanks comes the duty to safeguard what we have been given. We do this with humility and restraint. We should be humble knowing that our gift is undeserved. And we should be restrained as a way of treasuring our gifts. "We should thank God for beer and Burgundy," Chesterton adds, "by not drinking too much of them." Giving thanks is an expression of gratitude, but it also unlocks the door to humility and restraint. It is like saying, "How good of God to give me all these wonderful things that give me a sense of happiness". I have done nothing to deserve them, but I will cherish them and make sure that I use them as God intended.

Giving thanks can be a personal matter that is expressed on a moment to moment basis. But it is also a worthwhile and laudable thing that it be celebrated nationally on an annual basis and in a more formal way. The fourth Thursday of November became Thanksgiving's official Federal holiday in 1863 when Abraham Lincoln proclaimed a national day of "Thanksgiving and Praise to our beneficent Father who dwelleth in the Heavens." This was an extraordinary gesture by America's 16th president inasmuch as it was made during the Civil War. Even during the darkest hours, we can find something that can elicit our thanks. The document was written by Secretary of State, William Seward, in which he fervently implored "the interposition of the Almighty Hand to heal the wounds of the nation and to restore it as soon as may be consistent with the Divine purposes of peace, harmony, tranquility and Union." Giving thanks is also about having hope, for we do not believe that the gifts that God has bequeathed to us will be His last.

On May 4, 2014, Pope Francis offered a Mass of Thanksgiving for Saint John Paul II's canonization. In his homily, referring to the Church's new saint, he remarked that "In the moments of sadness and of dejection, when everything seemed lost, he never lost hope, because his faith and hope were fixed on God." May all of our thanksgivings be crowned by this kind of hope.

THE MYSTERY OF THE HEART

In his book, *Prayer*, Hans Urs von Balthasar makes an arresting statement: "Man is the being who bears in his heart a mystery greater than himself." This is a statement that is rich in implication and warrants further explication. At first, it appears to be a contradiction. How can a liter carton of milk, for example, contain within itself more than a liter? How can anything, for that matter, be more than it is? The spiritual dimension, however, cannot be understood by a mathematical approach. The fact that the human heart can contain something greater than the person, although a mystery, is not a contradiction.

Our individuality is most evident to us, as attested by our powerful instinct for self-preservation. No one has to explain our individuality to us. It is the most immediately obvious aspect of our existence. But there is far more to us than our individuality. If we live as mere individuals, roaming in the midst of strangers, we radically short change ourselves. This is why narcissism, hedonism, and materialism fail to satisfy the whole person. Excessive preoccupation with individuality leads to the unrealistic notion that we can be *autonomous*, wholly independent on others, self-sufficient.

The heart symbolizes the moral and spiritual center of our

lives. The *Book of Proverbs* enjoins us to "Keep thy heart with all diligence; for out of it are the issues of life" (iv. 23). The Greeks had three words for life. *Bios* refers to individual biological life; *psuche* refers to the conscious life of the individual. *Zoe* refers to life that transcends mere individuality, whether biological or psychological. It refers to life that can be shared. This notion of *zoe* was essential for Christianity since Christ's life is shared with others, and Christians are commanded to share their lives with their neighbors. *Zoe* means that there is in each human being, the "heart" if we need a name, which is greater than individuality and can be shared with others as well as with God. *Zoe* makes prayer not only a possibility but a personally fulfilling.

Jacques Maritain offers a penetrating insight into the dynamic of the *zoe* life of the heart. He states that when we get in touch with this deeper dimension of our being—the mystery of the heart, in von Balthasar's words—we find that we "superexist". At this moment, "the Self is transfigured" and we discover "the basic generosity of existence". Then, as Maritain goes on to explain, we realize "that love is not a passing pleasure or emotion, but the very meaning of {our} being alive" (*Existence and the Existent*, pp. 89-90). The purpose of life, therefore, is to give. We find ourselves when we discover that the meaning of our lives is to give of ourselves.

We find physical counterparts that attest to our nature as lovers and givers. A woman's uterus and her breast milk are not there for her own individual benefit. They exist to receive and nourish the lives of others. In this regard, they represent something greater than herself and fit smoothly into the notion that the essential purpose of life is to give. And this is why, "it is better to give than to receive".

Von Balthasar's statement has direct reference to prayer, though it is equally applicable to the nature of the human being as capable of superexisting. The heart is, to use a mechanical image, a kind of radio receiving set that, when it is turned on, is tuned to God. Prayer is a dialogue. We could not receive God's initial signal if we did not possess an inner ability that is designed to receive it. One cannot knock on the door if there is no door to receive the knock. But in addition to receiving God's Word, our heart functions as a kind of transmitter, capable of answering it. Autonomous man is a myth; man is meant to engage in prayer with God and to share the love in his heart with others. It is far better to strive for magnanimity than to be lured by the mirage of autonomy.

WHY DO WE SING?

"Singing," wrote St. Isidore, in his *Etymologies*, "lightens weariness in solitary tasks". This very human activity seems to be as natural and rejuvenating as breathing. This is evident in children who happily go about singing long before they know a song to sing or any lyrics to accompany it. "The only thing better than singing," said songstress Ella Fitzgerald, "is more singing". For Andrea Bocelli, "Singing provides a true sense of lightheartedness. If I sing when I am alone, I feel wonderful. It's freedom". And, as someone once said, "Singing is the celebration of oxygen".

"I sing of arms and the man," (*Arma virumque cano*) is how Virgil opened *The Aeneid*, Book I. Many public events have opened with Samuel Francis Smith's immortal words, "My country 'tis of thee, sweet land of liberty, of thee I sing". In 1932, George Gershwin's *Of Thee I Sing* was the first musical to win a Pulitzer Prize for drama. We sing prior to an important athletic contest and sing our children to sleep. Opera is the grand art of communicating only in song. Singing is the romantic gift of the troubadours and the instinctive expression of birds. The *Song of Songs* blends earthly and divine love.

Perhaps the highest form of singing is in prayer. And if Thomas Day's book, *Why Catholics Can't Sing*, is anywhere close to the mark, Catholics could do a better job of melding their prayers to song. *Psalm 95* states, "O come, let us sing unto the Lord: let us heartily rejoice in the strength of our salvation." *Psalm* 98 reads, "O sing unto the Lord a new song: for he hath done marvelous things".

A phrase attributed to St. Augustine—"He who sings prays twice"--has taken on the status of a timeless adage. The Latin has an internal rhyme that lends it a certain musical charm: *Qui bene cantat bis orat.* The Bishop of Hippo may have said this, but it is nowhere to be found in his written words that have come down to us. He did, nonetheless, link prayer to singing. "Singing belongs to one who loves" (*cantare amantis est*), he wrote. In addition, he stated that "He who sings praise, does not only praise, but also praises joyfully; he who sings praise, not only sings, but also loves Him to whom he is singing" (*Qui enim cantat laudem, non solum laudat, sed etiam hilariter laudat; qui cantat laudem, non solum cantat, sed et amat eum quem cantat*).

Christmas carols would be comparatively flat if they were merely recited and not sung. When people speak, they usually speak one person at a time. When they sing, they can sing in multitudes. We might say that "He who sings in a choir, sings thrice". The human heart bears a mystery that is greater than its possessor. When speech is elevated to song, more of our heart is involved, and that expression can have a special affinity with prayer. Music arises from the depths of the human heart. It is our answer to God's benevolence, our joyful and loving response to the Good News.

We sing because our hearts are bursting with joy, and mere speech cannot do justice to what we feel. We raise our voices in song to God in thanks for all He has given us. But we may also sing because we need to rise above the difficulties of life. In this regard, St. Augustine gives us some practical advice about singing, in one of his sermons (*Sermo 256*). "Let is sing *alleluia* here on earth, while we are still anxious and worrying, so that we may one day be able to sing it in heaven, without any worry or care." Bach, Handel and Mozart took this advice to heart. We sing because we need to allay our fears; we sing because we need to rehearse our role in the heavenly choir.

THE PLACE OF GOD

In the year 1979, the Academy of Motion Picture Arts and Sciences awarded Dustin Hoffman an Oscar for Best Actor for his role in *Kramer vs. Kramer*. The grateful recipient began his acceptance speech by saying, "I'd like to thank . . . (pregnant pause) . . . my parents for not practicing birth control." As expected, the line drew gales of laughter from the audience. It was as funny as it was unexpected. But it does bring to mind a flurry of more sober thoughts.

Contraception, by 1979, had become a first line of defense against unwanted pregnancies. Thanks to his parents avoiding such a pregnancy preventative, Mr. Hoffman's conception was not thwarted. The second line of defense is abortion. It would have been a *faux pas* of considerable magnitude if a future honoree would say, "I'd like to thank my parents for not aborting me." This line would not have drawn laughter. It would have rendered the audience most uncomfortable. Hollywood does not want to think of abortion as killing someone, especially a potential Oscar winner.

Dr. Alan Guttmacher and others, since the early 70's, have been trying to "detoxify" the word abortion of any negative implications it may contain. But it remains an ugly word and continues to provoke disturbing feelings. It is the reality that remains more powerful than the word, even when it is sweetened by the euphemism "choice".

At another time and in a different milieu, an award winner might have thanked God for giving him life. The two lines of defense against life—contraception and abortion—shift the authorship of life away from God and to the parents. What a heavy responsibility it must be, though, to be the sole authors of life. Meditating on the effects of contraception, the well-known psychotherapist, Rollo May, has put it this way: "For no longer does 'God' decide we are to have children; we do. And who has even begun to comprehend the meaning of that tremendous fact?"

Saint John Paul II has drawn attention to the two radically different meanings of the word "my". It is a difference that parallels the Latin Possessive and Partitive genitives. When I say, "This is my pen," I mean that I own the pen and that in doing so I am not infringing on any rights the pen might have. In other words, I *possess* the pen. On the other hand, when I say, "This is my country," it is clear that I am not claiming ownership of the country, but merely indicating that I belong to the country as a *part* of it.

If God is the author of life, then parents do not *possess* their children, but are stewards entrusted to care for them. A great deal of anxiety is allayed when parents understand that they are working together with the Author of life and have not taken on the burden of raising children solely on their own. Contraception and abortion have a way of eclipsing God, and turning children into objects of parental ownership.

Rollo May has observed, in therapy, particularly among professional people, that parents who have had their one child assume a great temptation to overprotect that child. The burden placed on the child, according to Professor May, is "like a prince born into a royal family", carrying "a weight for which children were never made." The child, of course, has his own destiny, one that is known better to God than to mom or dad.

The Pontifical Council for the Family issued a "Charter of the Rights of the Family" in 1983. It underscores the primary significance of God in overseeing marriage and the family: "The Catholic Church, aware that the good of the person, of society, and of the Church herself passes by way of the family, has always held it part of her mission to proclaim to all the plan of God instilled in human nature concerning marriage and the family, to promote these two institutions and to defend them against all those who attack them."

Contraception and abortion contravene God's plan. They tend to create a mentality in which parents assume their roles more as possessors or owners of their children rather than as guardians or stewards. We are right to thank our parents for their role in giving us life, but the highest thanks should be reserved for God. God's place should remain paramount.

POPE JOHN II DAY FOR CANADA

Canada has passed legislation making April 2 Pope John Paul II Day. Bill C-266 passed on December 16 and has received royal assent. The law's preamble praises the long-serving pope and canonized saint for his "vital role in promoting international understanding and peace," his inspiration of youth, his visits to Canada (especially for World Youth Day in 2002), and his leadership in the struggle "to end communism in Europe".

Wladyslaw Lizon, a Toronto-based Conservative MP, who introduced the Bill, commented that "Pope John Paul II presented a valuable message of courage, a defense of freedom and profound statements of hope and commitment to all people". 217 members of parliament supported the bill, while 42—all New Democrats—voted against it. Lizon pointed out that "Pope John Paul II proved that nothing is impossible. He stood up for populations that were oppressed by totalitarian regimes. He will be remembered for his role in the collapse of several stifling dictatorships, and for the way he inspired peaceful opposition to Communism in Poland, leading to its eventual collapse in Central and Eastern Europe."

Saint John Paul II was truly a man for all people, despite what his critics, who did not fully understand the Pontiff's message, claimed. In rural Kenya, for example, thousands of children—plus many cats, roosters, and even hotels—are named John Paul. When *Time* magazine named him "Man of the Year," for 1994, the editors had this to say: "In a year when so many people lamented the decline in moral values or made excuses for bad behavior, Pope John Paul II forcefully set forth his vision of the good life and urged the world to follow it. For such rectitude—or recklessness, as his detractors would have it—he is *Time's* Man of the Year."

"Recklessness," is the accusation made by those who wanted him to be less Catholic than he was and approve abortion, contraception, women's ordination, and same-sex marriage. The word better describes the accusers since John Paul would have been just another layman had he abandoned Catholic teaching for the sake of political popularity. John Paul's greatness lies in his fidelity, consistency, integrity, courage, and love, an array of qualities rarely, if ever, found together in a politician. The Dalai Lama had expressed his admiration for John Paul's character and commitment with a touch of sympathy: "He really has a will and a determination to help humanity through spirituality. That is marvelous. That is good. I know how difficult it is for leaders on these issues." Another non-Catholic, Billy Graham, said that John Paul will go down in history as the greatest of our modern Popes. He's been the strong conscience of the whole Christian world."

John Paul's religiosity did not compromise his humanity, but strengthened it. He was a humanitarian in the truest sense of the term. "Humanity should question itself," he remarked," about the absurd and always unfair phenomenon of war, on whose stage of death and pain only remain standing the negotiating table that could and should have prevented it." Nor did his religiosity interfere with his appreciation of science. "Science can purify religion from error and superstition," he wrote. "Religion can purify science from idolatry and false absolutes."

All great men are misunderstood by some who are less than

great. Pope John Paul II Day is a fitting tribute to a true humanitarian, an apostle of peace, a witness to hope, and a man of God. Canadians should welcome this legislation with open minds and with open hearts. Honoring his Day in the future, assures that Canadians will continue to draw from his rich legacy, especially his love for humanity.

—PART TEN—
LIFE AND CHRISTMAS

"The best Christmas of all is the presence of a family
all wrapped up with each other."
– Anonymous

CHRISTMAS AND THE
VIEW FROM ETERNITY

Perhaps the two most beloved Christmas stories that we see every year on television are Charles Dickens' *A Christmas Carol* and Frank Capra's *It's A Wonderful Life*. The former involves a man from Hell, Jacob Marley, who shows Ebenezer Scrooge the ruinous future he is preparing for himself and for others. The latter involves an angel from heaven, Clarence Odbody, who shows George Bailey what a wonderful life he has had. In both stories the order of time is changed so that the trajectory of the two lives can be seen from the perspective of eternity. Also central to the stories are the families of Bob Cratchit and George Bailey. Each person can have a profound effect on others, especially on intimates, according to how he views the significance of his life.

Christmas is about eternity since it represents the eternal God coming into a world of time. It is the conjunction between the timeless and the temporal. It offers us, therefore, an occasion to reflect on our lives and consider where we are going. It beckons us to see our lives in a larger perspective and to think about the relationship between our birth and our destiny. Christ's birth is inseparable from his destiny. The light He brings into the world is one that illuminates all of human history.

This larger perspective, achieved at Christmas time in both

of these timeless stories, is needed for the conversions of the two central characters. Given a frame of reference that transcends the moment, they come to realize the essential importance of love and generosity. They come to understand that life is a blessing, one that must be shared with others. Both the Bailey and the Cratchit families are the immediate beneficiaries of this insight. They are the beneficiaries of what the Holy Family represents.

Christmas, as we know only too well, is a time of gift-giving. This popular practice, however, has been roundly criticized for commercializing a holy occasion. But gifts can transcend commercialization when they are given in the right spirit. They should be gentle reminders that the greatest of all gifts is the gift of life, one that was threatened on the first Christmas by King Herod. The gift we give is finite and limited. They often fail to last a year. But what they should symbolize is far more. They should say, "This gift in itself is merely a token. On a deeper level it says that I am happy you are here and I want this gift to enhance your life, make you happy, and remind you that you are part of a loving family, a loving community."

Gifts should elicit thanks. The reason Christmas presents are wrapped is so that the beneficiary can say, "Thank you" twice. The initial thank you may be more pure than the second because it is said without knowing exactly what the wrapped package contains. The sight of a myriad of presents at the foot of the Christmas tree is an image that fills us with expectation, the anticipation that packaged love will inspire grateful hearts.

The gifts of the Magi have spiritual significance that symbolizes the eternal. Gold honors his kingship, frankincense celebrates his deity, and myrrh (an embalming oil) refers to His death. These gifts proclaim the eternal significance of Christmas because Christ's kingship is everlasting, because He is God, and because He was destined to rise from the dead.

Christmas expands our hearts and minds as it unites us with

an eternal plan. The two aforementioned stories stir our hearts because they offer us credible tales of how Christmas is not simply about having a good time, but of having a wonderful life.

CHRISTMAS AS A TRANSFORMATION

There are Revolutions, and there are Transformations. A Revolution, in the dictionary's first meaning of the word, makes a full circle and always returns to where it began. And that is why such Revolutions always fail to improve things. But even those Revolutions that seek radical change oftentimes follow a similar circular pattern, according to the French proverb, *Plus ça change, plus c'est la même chose* (The more things change, the more they stay the same). A Transformation, on the other hand, such as what Christianity represents, brings life closer to God and carries with it a universal blessing. Christmas, the birth of Christianity, presents us with a Transformation for the good, the true, and the beautiful. It is "progressive" in the best sense of the word.

In his "Theology of the Body," Saint John Paul II writes about three revolutionary figures that he refers to as *The Masters of Suspicion*: Sigmund Freud, Karl Marx, and Friedrich Nietzsche. The revolutionary ideas of this triumvirate created a great deal of noise and commotion in the modern world, but they failed to benefit humanity. John Paul associated them, respectively, with the three sins that John the Evangelist describes in his *First Letter* (2:15-17): the "lust of the flesh," the "lust of the eyes," and the "pride of life". Freud wanted to free the sexual instinct from

185

conventional restrictions. He represents *lust*. Marx encouraged the proletariat to revolt so that they could gain the material possessions that they coveted. He stands for *avarice*. Nietzsche welcomed the cultivation of an ego too powerful to be kept in check by an oppressive god. He symbolizes *pride*. The Deadly Sins of lust, envy, and pride have never advanced the cause of humanity.

Christmas represents a Transformation of incomparable power and magnitude. It transforms lust into chastity, avarice into generosity, and pride into humility. The thinking of Freud, Marx, and Nietzsche has been thoroughly discredited. They have had their day. No one ever honors Freud by memorializing, each year, his birth in Vienna. Christmas, chastely honors a babe born in swaddling clothes who is placed in a manger. No one ever commemorates the eve of Marx's birth by hanging stockings by the fireplace anticipating a generosity that he never exhibited. Christmas welcomes the generosity that pours from people's hearts in the form of gifts of all kinds. No one ever remembers Nietzsche's philosophy each year by singing songs of praise to himself. Christmas offers the humble image of children singing carols while standing in the snow and braving winter's cold. Christmas is about peace and love. But it is also about chastity, generosity, and humility.

The Transforming power of Christmas is beautifully and convincingly displayed in film. Consider the following: *It's A Wonderful Life, Miracle on 34th Street, The Holly and the Ivy, The Magic Christmas Tree, 'Twas the Night Before Christmas, The Gift of the Magi, Christmas Story, Holiday Inn, Nutcracker Fantasy, I'll Be Home for Christmas, An Old Fashioned Christmas, White Christmas*, and *A Christmas Carol*. A story is immediately transformed and illuminated whenever Christmas is depicted on the screen. It invariably expresses something other-worldly, yet more satisfying and salutary than what the world itself can confer. It brings a joy to the screen and a sense of hope, however brief, to the viewers.

The unique transforming power of Christmas will continue to radiate its grace until the end of time. There is nothing else to which it can be compared. Secular "holidays" are really not "holy days" at all, but poor imitations of what a holy day truly represents. Therefore, Christmas reminds us of what is holy. And holiness is that undefiled purity that we need to experience as often as we can so that we do not conform too unreservedly to an unholy world. Christmas reminds us of who we are and the nature of our destiny. A holy Christmas is also a merry one since it is not possible to be holy without being happy.

WHAT THE ANIMALS
KNEW AT CHRISTMAS

You may have wondered, and rightly so, why the ox and the ass appear so often beside the Christ child in various images of the Nativity. These two rather disparate animals frequently appear in Catholic medieval paintings of Christ's birth, and nearly all the Orthodox icons of the first Christmas. Yet, they are not mentioned in the New Testament narratives. Nonetheless, even in the earliest example of a nativity scene known to us, a swaddled babe in flanked, not by Mary and Joseph, but by the ox at his head and the ass at his feet.

Apocryphal texts, such as the pseudo-Matthew, record these animals worshipping the Christ child. Also, in what seems to be an Arabic translation of Habakkuk 3:2, the prophet states, "Between two animals you are made manifest." Although these texts may not be authentic, they nonetheless add weight to the legend.

The most important and reliable Biblical text, Isaiah 1:3, makes it clear that the ox and the ass are not present in the manger scene to provide atmosphere or as the product of a pious imagination. According to the great prophet, "An ox knows its owner, an ass, its master's manger; but Israel does not know, my people has not understood." This text makes it clear that the ox and ass know something very important that even many human beings do not know, namely, who their Master is. This resonates with Christ's question to Simon Peter: "But who do you say that I am?" Peter does answer correctly and is rewarded by being given the keys of the kingdom of heaven, and made the Church's first pope (Matthew: 16: 16-19).

Pope Benedict XVI includes a chapter called, "Ox and Ass Know Their Lord," in his book, *The Blessing of Christmas* (Ignatius Press, 2007). "It is striking to note," he writes, in the medieval pictures of Christmas how the artists give the two animals almost human faces and how they stand before the mystery of the child and bow down in awareness and reverence." According to the former Pontiff, this makes sense because "we are but oxen and asses vis-à-vis the Eternal God, oxen and asses whose eyes are opened on Christmas night, so that they can recognize their Lord in the crib". The birth of Christ opens our eyes so that we come to know who our real Master is and it is not wealth, power, status, or pleasure.

A second important point is brought out in Deuteronomy 22:12, where we read: "You shall not plow with an ox and an ass harnessed together." According to dietary proscriptions in the Old Testament, the ox was considered to be a "clean" animal while the ass was regarded as "unclean". Also, the ox was seen as representing Israel whereas the ass symbolized the Gentiles. Biblical scholars have explained the presence of the ox and the ass at Christmas as Christ joining factors that are usually regarded as extremes. Therefore, the birth of Christ is the union of the spiritual and the corporeal, the clean and the unclean, the uncreated and the created, the human and the divine, heaven and earth, time and eternity.

Christmas is about a birth. But more importantly, it is about opening our eyes to our true Master who has widened our perspective on life, showing us that there is far more to our lives than what we can find immediately around us, and that we have much

greater capacities for love and peace than we could ever have imagined. May this Christmas be your happiest and most meaningful.

MY FIVE CHRISTMAS GIFTS

If prayer and pen can conjure up a gift, I would like to utilize this possibility and provide five Christmas gifts for my faithful readers of The Wanderer. These "gifts" would be of an intellectual nature, "lights," as it were, consistent with the "Five Mysteries of Light" that Saint John Paul II added to the Rosary.

Christmas centers on a Light that dispels darkness and illumines the mind and heart so that the message of Jesus can be more clearly discerned. My "gifts," therefore, are intended to illuminate five areas of darkness that have clouded certain truths of the Catholic faith. My hope is that these "gifts," which are merely re-statements of enduring truths, will be treasured and not exchanged for something more trendy. Or to put it another way, there are a few lights on the Christmas tree that are flickering. All they need is a little tightening so that they can shine again with their original unwavering brightness.

1) Religion protects and cultivates spirituality:

The secular world is in love with spirituality. It is religion that it objects to. Thus, we find prevalent in our society a false dichotomy between spirituality and religion. The heretical belief has been well circulated that organized religion stifles spirituality. The problem with unorganized spirituality, however, is that it soon becomes disorganized spirituality. No one exclaims, "I love baseball, but I don't like organized baseball; structure is spoiling the game, there are too many rules." A vital function of Catholicism, as a religion, is to test and clarify spirituality to ensure that it is directed to God and in harmony with the needs of one's neighbor. Religion is to spirituality what music is to dancing, engineering is to mathematics, and what a directed life is to a series of momentary impulses.

2) Catholicism teaches truth:

Do Catholic churches need to make available material that promotes abortion, same-sex marriage, human cloning, and so forth, so that churchgoers can become acquainted with the "other side"? The "other side" is represented adequately enough by incessant reiterations through the Media and other highly visible avenues of secular culture. Churches have a duty to represent the truth of Church teachings. They have no need of either sleeping with the enemy or having the enemy sleep with them. When a math teacher explains that $2 + 2 = 4$, he incurs no responsibility to represent contradictory viewpoints. Adam and Eve may have been better off had they not considered the viewpoint of the Serpent. It is by the light of truth that we are freed. The "other side" is the dark side. And, in the words of St. Paul, "Light and darkness have nothing in common".

3) Catholics are fundamentally humanists:

Secular journalists never tire of complaining that Catholics are forever trying to "impose" their faith values on the public. But

192

Catholics do not try to impose Sunday Mass, Ash Wednesday abstinence, and Holy Days of Obligation—which are faith-based—on non-Catholics. In fact, they could not "impose" any values on anyone, even if their lives depended on it. Values are intrinsically non-imposable. Moral issues, such as abortion and euthanasia, however, are broader, more humanistic concerns. Catholic morality is not strictly a matter of faith, but reason's response to the natural law. It is through the universal faculty of reason that Catholics embrace all other human beings. We all begin at ground zero. Issues involving human rights are not narrowly Catholic, but represent a convergence that unites all human beings. Catholic morality is simply anthropology put into practice. Catholics *impart* truths; they do not *impose* them.

4) The dogma is the drama:

Dogma, which simply refers to teaching, is neither stifling nor a barrier to creativity. Without dogma the Church would be devoid of content and, as a result, be both unhelpful as well as unintelligible. She would have no stories to warm the heart, no lamps to light the way. According to Church dogma, man is able to know something about God though this knowledge is infinitely less than what God is in Himself. Consequently, there is endless opportunity for creativity, as man navigates from the finite toward the infinite. A ship, thanks to her navigational instruments, can explore no end of hitherto unknown regions. But take away these instruments, and the ship is lost. Just as the light from the North Star guides the ship, Church dogma gives us the confidence that our voyage has meaning and direction. The dogma, then, like any good adventure, is the drama.

5) Christ must come first:

Everyone wants peace. But how many are willing to pay the price? Peace is not simply an object of choice. It is the fortuitous consequence of choosing to live life well. If I put myself first, I inevitably find myself in conflict with all others, especially those who put themselves first. My ego is no more spacious than itself and can hardly be a peace formula for as small a multitude as two, let alone all the people in the world. Christ's way of love and truth embraces all mankind. Without Him, as John the Evangelist tells us, we can do nothing. The formula for JOY is to put Jesus first, others second, and yourself third. "Thy will be done" is a simple, prayerful acknowledgement of the primacy of Christ, who is, *par excellence*, the Prince of Peace.

THE WHITE HOUSE'S
FIRST CHRISTMAS TREE

The First of a series of important events—the First solo flight across the Atlantic Ocean, the First landing on the moon, the First Thanksgiving—holds an honored place in the human memory and in the bank of history. The First Christmas Tree in the White House was very special, not only because it inaugurated an esteemed tradition, but what it meant to America's First Lady.

Two months before the inauguration of Franklin Pierce, America's 14th president, his only surviving child, Bennie, age eleven, was killed in a railroad accident. Jane Appleton Pierce, whose two other sons died in early childhood, fell into a deep melancholy. She did not attend her husband's inauguration. In fact, she wanted nothing to do with Washington, D.C. Becoming "First Lady" meant nothing to her in the face of lost motherhood. Her grief, despite her abiding Christian faith, like that of Rachel, could not be consoled.

Rather than join her husband in Washington, Mrs. Pierce remained in Boston and did not leave for several days. Friends convinced her that she should join her husband in the nation's capitol. She traveled as far as Baltimore, but stayed there for several weeks. President Pierce visited her there as often as he could. At last, he was able to persuade her to accompany him back to Washington.

Poor Mrs. Pierce, the "very picture of melancholy," as one person described her, had staterooms at the White House draped in black in honor of Bennie. She refused to take part in any political functions and secluded herself in two rooms on the second floor where she spent much of her time writing long letters to her lost child. She would give the letters to Sidney Webster, confidential secretary to the president, who would routinely promise to "get them in the mail right away". She came to exemplify, according to Washington gossips, "The Shadow of the White House."

The First Lady's unrelieved, dark mood was, naturally, of great concern to her husband as well as to White House staff members. Sidney Webster, together with some of his co-workers, hoping to bring some cheer into the life of Mrs. Pierce, came up with a bold, though psychologically risky, idea. They would arrange for a Christmas tree to be set up inside the White House and a group of youngsters to sing carols. With the president's approval, the plan went ahead. It would all be, they hoped and prayed, for Mrs. Pierce's benefit.

On the morning of Christmas Eve, the president's grieving wife was led downstairs by her husband to the door of the East Room. As the door opened, boys and girls from the New York Avenue Presbyterian Church began singing "Away in a Manger."

Jane Pierce, completely taken by surprise, wept so vigorously that she shook. As she began to regain her composure, she became entranced by the brightly decorated tree and was beguiled by the children raising their voices in honor of a Savior born in a manger.

According to Washington chronicles, Jane Appleton Pierce then produced the first radiant smile that anyone in the capitol had ever seen flash upon her face. "Thank you, boys and girls, for your beautiful carols," she said. "Keep your places, please, while Mr. Snow [the informal chief of staff] goes to see what sweetmeats Cook has made ready for your visit." Turning to her husband and still radiant with surprise and joy, she embraced him and exclaimed: "Thank you, Mr. Pierce, for the most wonderful Christmas tree in the world. Best of all, Bennie is looking down from heaven and is enjoying it with us. That means I won't even have to write him a letter to describe it! Thank you for the most wonderful Christmas surprise I ever had!"

One cannot underestimate the value that the grace of the Christmas Season and the countless expressions of peace bring to people of good will. Honoring the babe born in Bethlehem in decoration and in song provides an unfailing benediction. The First Christmas Tree in the White House, in 1856, may have proven to have been the most salutary.

www.ingramcontent.com/pod-product-compliance
Lightning Source LLC
Chambersburg PA
CBHW022006090426
42741CB00007B/917